Brave Dreams:
A Season in the Atlanta Braves' Farm System

Bill Ballew

A Division of Howard W. Sams & Company
A Bell Atlantic Company

Published by Masters Press
A Division of Howard W. Sams & Company, A Bell Atlantic Company
2647 Waterfront Pkwy E. Dr, Suite 300, Indianapolis, IN 46214

Printed in the United States of America.

96 97 98 99 00 01 10 9 8 7 6 5 4 3 2 1

Library of Congress Cataloging-in-Publication Data

Brave Dreams: A Year in the Atlanta Braves' Farm System / Bill Ballew
p. cm.
ISBN: 1-57028-081-9: $14.95

Information Pending

Dedication

To Hope and Brad, the lights of my life.

Credits

Front Cover Photo © Richmond (Va.) Times-Dispatch
Back Cover Photo © Richmond Braves
Cover Design by Kelli Ternet
Photo reproduction assistance by Terry Varvel and Scott Stadler
Edited by Kim Heusel
Text layout by Leah Marckel

Table Of Contents

Preface

For my money, there is no better entertainment value than a night at a minor-league ballpark. For three or four dollars a person, on average one-third the cost of a major-league ticket, fans can enter a baseball temple, sit close to the action, still afford a couple of beers and a souvenir or two, and watch young players hone their skills while trying to work their way to one of the most lucrative professions our country offers.

Unbeknownst to most of the patrons at the more than 150 minor-league venues throughout the United States are the trials and tribulations the field's participants endure over the course of a season. The mind games and politics they encounter, the pressure and beat-the-clock mentality they face are often unseen by those who toil daily in offices and factories. At the same time, few if any of the players would trade places with those in the working world. They are living a dream, trying their best to make it a fairy tale instead of a nightmare.

That's what this book is about, dreams and the challenges players in one particular farm system, the Atlanta Braves, faced throughout one entire season. The team, in this case the world champions for the 1995 campaign, is merely an example, for the same things occur in all 28 organizations throughout professional baseball. In fact, in my opinion, the Braves are unrivaled in terms of how well they treat their players. Still, the system is set up so that most players wind up tasting more disappointment than success. It's survival of the fittest, with only the winners reaching the game's top level, the major leagues.

There have been countless books written about the minors in recent years. Most efforts have centered on the unique — outstanding achievements, unusual occurrences and other odd claims to fame. A few have been travelogues throughout certain parts of the country or one-season looks at one particular minor-league team. Many of those books I consider to be among my favorite works. Yet none has taken a complete look at an entire farm system and explored the yearlong effects trying to climb the ladder has on the organization's players. Until now.

As cliché as it may sound, this book of dreams is a dream itself. And the realization of this dream has come about due to the help of numerous individuals. Naturally the players, managers and coaches profiled within deserve the most credit. The same holds true for the Braves' minor-league office, most notably Chuck LaMar, now with the expansion Tampa Bay Devil Rays, Rod Gilbreath, Bobby Dews, Paul Snyder, Bobbie Cranford, Linda Smith and Lena Burney. The employees of the minor-league teams also came through in the clutch, including all the general managers and their employees, among them Matt Garvey, Sean O'Connor, Mark Hauser, Eric Johnson, Steve Barden, Jim Tessmer, Brad Cork and Leisha Cowart. Also helping out with pictures and other various needs were John Atkinson, Kyle York, Karl Lyles, Larry Ward and Alan Schwarz. Inspiration cannot be overlooked, and Rick Wolff deserves as much as anyone in that area.

Of course, my wife, Hope, was my greatest supporter, for she had to endure constant doubts and concerns, even while pregnant through most of the 1994 baseball season. Without her, this book would not exist.

Finally, many thanks go to the editorial staff at Masters Press, particularly Holly Kondras and Kim Heusel, who helped mold the raw but promising copy into major-league material.

Bill Ballew

Introduction

Gentle breezes wafted below pastel blue skies and cooled the early rays of the invigorating sun that soaked into the manager's weather-worn face. Sitting cross-legged on the dugout bench at West Palm Beach's Memorial Stadium, Bobby Cox appeared to feel as one with the setting while conveying thoughts of the situation at hand.

"Isn't this weather fantastic?" said Cox, who welcomed the warm air after spending most of the rainy winter in Atlanta recovering from knee replacement surgery on both legs. "I got up early this morning and you could see the sun climb over the water. It was simply beautiful. Damn, what a great day!"

Relaxed. Gradual. Anticipatable. In many ways, returning to spring training in Florida feels like the first day of school. The hard-core activity still a few weeks away, veteran players spend most of their time renewing friendships from previous years and forming acquaintances with the new arrivals. Lockers are assigned; supplies are distributed. The greatest difference from school comes in the way the participants arrive, driving up in models from Mercedes, Jaguar and Infiniti instead of riding shotgun in wood-paneled Ford station wagons and smoking yellow school buses.

"Hey, man, we got to go see T.P.," said rookie Tony Tarasco, wrapping his arm around the shoulders of a white, graying thirtysomething writer while moving toward the locker of third baseman Terry Pendleton.

"T.P., this dude look like a rapper?" Tarasco began. "He sure don't look like no rapper, but look at the shoes, the rubber toes!"

The topic centered on the writer's adidas Superstars, shoes that peaked in popularity during the 1970s prior to enjoying a revival among a certain musical sect more than 15 years later.

"Ain't no way he's a rapper," responded Pendleton, feigning disgust and waving the two away.

Such innocent bantering is a constant in clubhouses throughout professional baseball. The reason for its existence is, not unlike the school year, the baseball season evolves into an enervating and invigorating journey, featuring numerous peaks and valleys for even the most successful clubs. Humor creates a pecking order and relieves the stresses incurred over seven-plus months of togetherness. Find a clubhouse without practical jokes and other forms of tomfoolery and a slew of digits in the loss column will likely be present as well.

Throughout all 28 spring training camps strewn across Florida and Arizona, light-hearted humor is traditionally second only to optimism in terms of ubiquity, even among those teams that will discover a severe lack of prosperity before May is history. In West Palm Beach, prior to the 1994 season, a buoyancy that bordered on overweening emitted from everyone associated with the Atlanta Braves. Winners of three consecutive National League Western Division flags, the Atlanta players, coaches and front office staff exuded an attitude that anything short of a World Series title for the coming season would be considered failure.

Even Cox appeared relaxed. The 52-year-old skipper with the permanent close-mouthed smile knew his team had as much talent as any in the major leagues. The only things separating him from a pair of World Series rings were a baserunning gaffe in Minnesota in 1991 and four one-run defeats to Toronto in 1992. But during March, those horrifying events were simply aging memories that gave way to optimism and hope.

Forty players stretched on the damp outfield grass while Cox lauded the weather. Among those competing for the 25 major-league roster spots were some of the game's most accomplished players. A couple jobs were available, including one in left field, where four rookies — Chipper Jones, Ryan Klesko, Mike Kelly and Tarasco — were competing. That foursome joined first-year catcher Javy Lopez and no fewer than nine veterans who were products of the Atlanta farm system, thought by most observers as the game's best at developing major-league players.

While some teams had neglected their farm systems in recent years because of an absence of forward-thinking or the presence of a win-at-all-costs philosophy that sacrificed the future for the present, the Braves invested an average of $9 million annually to the scouting, signing and developing of selected high school and college players. The payoff was the premier organization in baseball, formulated with a recipe of home-grown talent, veterans acquired in trades for disposable minor-leaguers and a small group of hand-picked free agents.

Such an evaluation would have been considered ludicrous a half-decade earlier. Other than divisional championships in 1969 and 1982, both of which proved to be more deceptive than realistic in terms of long-term achievement, the Braves spent their first quarter-century after their 1966 move from Milwaukee to Atlanta serving as the doormat of the National League.

The root of the team's annual struggles involved the lack of a prosperous farm system, resulting in a trail of tears long enough for several teams. In the 1970s and early 1980s, Atlanta cut corners every way imaginable in player development. For example, in September 1974, the team united with 16 other clubs and formed the Central Scouting Bureau, defined as "a cooperative organization designed to provide an effective and economical method to scout the nation's young baseball talent." While most of the other member clubs maintained some semblance of a scouting department, the Braves trimmed their hunting corps to six scouts. By contrast, the Braves in 1994 hired 61 scouts, men who covered every state, all of Latin America, as well as such foreign countries as Canada and Mexico, and the continents of Australia, Europe and South America.

Making matters worse in the 1970s was the team's lack of players and instructors. In 1994 the Braves fielded eight minor-league clubs (four full-season and four short-season teams), each with a manager and two or three coaches. Atlanta had but four farm teams in 1975, with only a skipper at each location to help the budding players. The Braves basically applied a shotgun system, implemented to the greatest of extremes.

"We were told to go out and do what we thought best," said Bobby Dews, Atlanta's current minor-league field coordinator who managed Class A Greenwood in 1975. "We didn't have any coaches. We didn't have any schedules. It was like taking out a junior high team, where the head coach tries to do his best by himself."

Another self-inflicted shot involved the organization's poor judgment. Refusing to adjust their long-held philosophy of grooming power hitters, the Braves wasted first-round draft picks during the late 1970s and early 1980s. Part of the directive came from Henry Aaron, who took control of the farm system in 1977. To his credit, Aaron did not want to be a front office figurehead upon accepting the job of director of player development a few months after he retired as the game's home run king in 1976. He was responsible for the infusion of youth, or lack thereof, in the Atlanta organization, hired all coaches and instructors, negotiated contracts with the players and went on the road to instruct young hitters. An impressionable and patient teacher, Aaron enjoyed helping the minor-leaguers, and honestly believed he could mold players who showed some power potential into major-league prospects. In fact, other than refusing to put a full-time emphasis on his job, his Achilles heel was his loyalty toward his pupils.

Few would-be prospects panned out, however. With minimal financial dedication to the minors and even less talent production, new Braves owner Ted Turner spent outrageous amounts of money on fallow free agents. This motley crew was handed to Cox, who first arrived in Atlanta from the New York Yankees in 1978. Cox managed to coax a pair of fourth-place finishes in 1980 and 1981 after dwelling in the cellar his first two seasons. Those results satisfied no one. A frustrated Cox was fired following the 1981 campaign, and soon found greener pastures as manager of the Toronto Blue Jays.

Cox's departure created a revolving door at the Braves' managerial helm. Former Atlanta catcher Joe Torre was hired at the demands of the starched shirts at Turner Broadcasting, only to be dumped after one first-place and two runner-up finishes in the division. Eddie Haas, the consummate minor-league manager who had consistently molded castoffs from other organizations into efficient professional players at Richmond, took over before receiving a pink slip 121 games into the 1985 season, further blackening the eye of the seemingly incompetent organization. Bobby Wine took the reins for the remainder of the campaign, then handed them to former Pittsburgh skipper Chuck Tanner the following spring.

With all the changes, the deterioration of the minor-league system continued unabated. Rather than starting from the bottom of the minors and working up, teaching and related techniques were determined at the major-league level and passed down. Every new Atlanta manager held different beliefs, leaving what few prospects existed with so many mixed and confusing signals that it was difficult to achieve anything substantial. Dissension quickly filtered throughout the organization, leaving a farm system comprised of minor-league journeymen on the upper-level rosters and more suspects than prospects at the lower levels dominated by a group of malcontents and finger-pointers, none of whom would ever contribute in the major leagues.

The situation being what it was, more than a few people wondered about the state of Cox's mental health after the 1985 season. Cox had just guided Toronto to its first American League East pennant, earning manager-of-the-year accolades along the way. Yet, instead of building on his accomplishments in Canada, he traded in his Blue Jays uniform for a suit and tie as general manager of the Braves. Considering his experience in Atlanta just a few years earlier, most observers thought a straitjacket would be more appropriate.

"Believe me, it was tough to leave an organization with people I respected and loved to work with," Cox said. "But this opportunity allowed me to be home and work at the same time. That was the only reason I came back."

Most people would have experienced second thoughts after joining the fray, yet Cox instilled a positive attitude into everything he handled. His evaluations led to Dews becoming minor-league field coordinator, freeing scouting director Paul Snyder from the day-to-day farm system chores that Aaron typically neglected to place more attention on beating the bushes for young talent. Cox also directed Snyder and his growing scouting staff to select and sign the best talent available in the annual amateur draft, regardless of cost. He placed greater emphasis on pitching and speed instead of on power hitters, and sought quality from quantity by expanding the farm system to eight affiliates.

In essence, everything the team had done for the past dozen or so years was now handled in the opposite manner. "The direction was to stay off the free-agent market, save our draft picks, and do and spend as much as we could with the minor-league system," Cox said.

By no means did Cox expect immediate returns. The Braves continued to struggle at the major-league level, with a fifth-place finish in 1987 serving as the high-water mark between 1986 and 1990. The lone luxury from the lack of success was accrued with high picks in the annual amateur draft. From 1986 to 1991, Atlanta never had a first-round selection lower than sixth.

Snyder did his job by drafting pitchers such as Steve Avery, Tom Glavine, Kent Mercker, Mike Stanton and Mark Wohlers, and top prospects including Jones and Klesko. Cox also built toward the future by trading established veterans, including the cancerous Doyle Alexander, for whom Cox stole a 20-year-old John Smoltz from Detroit.

By 1990, four years of partings, planning and patience provided some light at the end of the proverbial tunnel. Even though the Braves posted a mere 65-97 record during the season, the nucleus of success was emerging. A young pitching staff received on-the-job training, while David Justice garnered National League rookie-of-the-year honors. Manager Russ Nixon, who replaced Tanner early in 1988, lost control of the team by midseason, leading Cox to return to the dugout helm in June.

The end product, thanks primarily to the efforts of Cox, Snyder and Dews, was a young major-league roster and a farm system bursting at the seams with talent. What was needed was someone to help the Braves reach the next level. Cox admitted that the dual role of general manager and skipper was too much for one person, so team president Stan Kasten searched for a leader who could develop a winner using the fine mixture of home-grown talent and free agents. He found his man in John Schuerholz, general manager of the Kansas City Royals for the previous decade.

Similar to Cox five years earlier, Schuerholz, a Napoleonic leader with a brash personality and an intolerance for carelessness, was thought insane by his colleagues. And following Cox's lead, Schuerholz set out to make several changes, including the creation of a more positive, professional atmosphere. Donned in his signature suspenders and tailor-made suits, he implemented a dress code for his staff that would make IBM proud. Schuerholz also refurbished the offices, improved the ballpark with a new concessions area and arranged for the playing field at Atlanta-Fulton County Stadium to be the best grass surface in baseball.

One thing Schuerholz did not do was overhaul the front office. His changes were limited to bringing in former colleague Dean Taylor as assistant general manager, and Chuck LaMar as director of scouting and player development. No one completely lost his job, although Snyder was pushed aside after years of putting together the raw talent in Atlanta's minor leagues.

A few changes also were made in the farm system. With Cox, Snyder and Dews having filled the organization with quality players, Schuerholz and LaMar fine-tuned the minors by releasing many nonprospects. They also reduced the number of farm teams from eight to seven, eliminating Class A Burlington in the Midwest League.

With a .563 winning percentage, the Atlanta farm system posted the second-best record among the 26 minor-league organizations in 1991, the first year under the Schuerholz-LaMar helm. The credit, and rightfully so, was given to Cox and his staff. Yet, after the first successful season, LaMar made some changes within the system, many of which proved controversial and unpopular.

LaMar joined the Braves as a well-respected judge of talent but with a reputation for being exigent. Unlike his predecessors, LaMar is not a backslapper or a Southern conversationalist. And unlike many of his contemporaries, his baseball experience did not come as a professional player. LaMar coached two years at the high school level and five seasons in the college ranks before spending four years as a scouting supervisor for Cincinnati in the mid-1980s. Those jobs preceded a two-year stint as Pittsburgh's director of minor-league operations and his arrival in Atlanta.

Initially, LaMar's personality, so straight-forward that many people believe incorrectly that he possesses little sense of humor, did not mix well with several long-term members of the Atlanta organization. LaMar focused on results, not traditions. Therefore, with little production in recent years, five veteran scouts were not rehired at the end of the 1991 season. Former Atlanta pitcher and Richmond manager Phil Niekro turned down the R-Braves' job for

1992 because he and LaMar interacted on the level of oil and water. Macon manager Roy Matijka was also let go, while the other three coaches joined the ranks of the unemployed.

Regardless of how unpopular the moves may have been, the complaints were drowned out by the chanting, tomahawk-chopping Braves fans as the wins continued to accumulate two years later. The combination of superb drafts, progressing players, and emerging major-league prospects proved LaMar and Schuerholz had done their jobs as well as anyone in the game. LaMar was promoted to assistant general manager of player development prior to the 1994 campaign, which further established him as a general manager-in-waiting at the major-league level.

"Teams that can scout and sign and then develop players will always be the teams that can field the consistent winners at the major-league level," LaMar said while overseeing the activity taking place on three minor-league practice fields. "In the Braves' case, there's no question that we have gone from worst to first by signing and developing our own players. All good organizations in baseball have believed in that philosophy for years, that to win consistently, you have to have that young flow of talent coming up through the minor leagues."

That flow was more like an avalanche during the spring of 1994. Five rookies, each with at least one year of Triple-A seasoning under his belt, were making the final step to the majors. Schuerholz made room for the green peas with moves that had sparked heated debates on the radio talk shows over the winter, among them allowing starters Otis Nixon and an injured Ron Gant along with the catching platoon of Greg Olson and Damon Berryhill to leave without any compensation.

"A pipeline of talented young players not only feeds quality talent to your major-league team all the time, it also allows you to replace high-priced talent when it gets too costly or if you have a catastrophic injury like we've had," Schuerholz said.

Even with the many departures, a plethora of established talent still resided in Atlanta's major-league camp. Subsequently, no more than three spots on the major-league roster, two in long relief and another as a reserve outfielder, remained open for competition during the early stages of spring training.

Spring Fever

1

Dreams. Desire. Like the chicken and the egg, no one is exactly certain which begat the other. What is known is a large dose of both traits, regardless of the order, must be present in the heart and soul of every young man who plays baseball for pay.

Traditionally, these traits appear early in life. Every time a young boy opens a pack of cards, attends a game or receives his first glove, something unexplained takes place within the cortical functions of the brain. It alone isn't the sweet taste of bubble gum, the feel of supple, molded leather, the smell of fresh-cut grass, or the distinct sounds of popping mitts and pinging bats. Combined, and the sensations become overwhelming and intoxicating. "Dreams for sale" an unwritten sign must read someplace. The dream? To become the next American hero at the game's highest level. The price? Enough desire to pursue that dream until it ends in dust and disarray.

The process starts as soon as organized games can be played. The cream rarely takes long to rise to the top. Once puberty kicks in, physical maturity whittles the crop of dreamers multifold. When the high school, and in some cases, college, games begin, the dreams usually end. Those fortunate enough to remain in fantasy land do so with the help of representatives from the 28 major-league organizations, one of which offers the young man a paycheck for his baseball services between March and September, to see if his talents on the diamond can be parlayed into a job in the Show.

In order to make his dream become reality, a player must climb the hiring team's organizational ladder. Consisting of six to eight minor-league teams, located in towns and cities ranging in size from Princeton, West Virginia (population 7,000), to Phoenix, Arizona (2 million residents in the metropolitan area), the ladder is scaled from bottom to top, from rookie leagues to low Class A to high Class A to Double A to Triple A. The process is not elementary, nor does a player have it made once he climbs aboard the ladder. Folks back home will tell everyone that it's just a matter of time before Johnny Local plays in the big leagues. The truth is, at least 90 percent of the young men drafted to play professional baseball will see their dreams die hard as desires erode and disappear, buried in the dirt throughout distant fields in anonymous minor-league stomping grounds.

"When you're first in the minors, you're just happy to be playing pro ball," said outfielder Brian Kowitz. "After your first year or so, you kind of have a feel for what's going to happen, where you're going to be heading. It's a very insecure feeling, and it's not glamorous at all. You have control over what you're doing and that's it. But the front office can send you up, send you down, play you, bench you. Usually you don't know what's going to happen. You don't know how long you are going to be in one place. You just don't know."

No one should underestimate the power or the effect of dreams and desire. The bus travel, the fast food, the constant pressure, the daily grind, aspects that make minor-league baseball so challenging and arduous, all of which must be overcome in order to fulfill that dream. It is those types of conditions that create the high failure rate and produce a sense among the participants that the major leagues can at times be so close, yet so far away.

The entrance to the Atlanta clubhouse beneath the concrete Memorial Stadium stands in West Palm Beach is just an underhanded toss away from the minor-league complex. Divided only by a 3-foot-high chain-link fence with an unlocked gate, the twisted, diamond-shaped wire may as well be the Great Wall of China as far as the Braves' minor-leaguers are concerned.

"When I was in minor-league camp last year, it was like, 'Man, ain't no way I'll ever get over there,'" said 21-year-old pitcher Terrell Wade, experiencing his first spring with the major-league club in 1994. "The coaches said, 'Don't worry, it'll fall into place for you.' I said, 'I'm not worrying about it, I'm just saying...'"

For Atlanta's minor-league players, spring training consists of two locales: the Tommie Aaron Center at Memorial Stadium and the Ramada Inn hotel, located just beyond the complex's center field wall. And while the major-league players enjoy the life South Florida offers around the burdens of baseball, minor-leaguers must adhere to a list of rules that conjure up memories of summer camp.

Players are required to report to the ballpark every day, even when sick. Role call takes place every morning at 9:30, uniforms must be donned during workouts and no earrings can be worn while in uniform. At the hotel, curfew is 11 every evening. Players, who reside two to a room, may not change rooms or roommates without permission. Wives or girlfriends are not allowed. The hotel pool and bar are off-limits at all times.

Breakfast is served at 6:30, and dinner comes at 6:00, both at the hotel. Lunch, usually consisting of sandwiches, is available in the clubhouse. Players must sign in at the hotel restaurant, cannot wear tank tops, flip flops, hats or sunglasses, and must have a shirt with a collar, long pants and socks in order to be served the evening meal.

Despite the rules and regulations, most of which are standard throughout baseball, Atlanta's minor-leaguers reside in the lap of luxury when compared to their contemporaries in other organizations. "The food's great," said pitcher Aaron Turnier. "I got buddies in other organizations, and they get fed like they're in the Army. They rag on me, saying, 'You guys are always winning, you must be getting steak.' It really is good. The hotel is a nice place. The Braves take good care of us."

Terrell Wade's laid-back personality off the field often disguises his aggressive manner on the mound. (Photo courtesy of Richmond Braves)

However nice, those accommodations pale in comparison to what the major-leaguers are offered at the Palm Beach Gardens Marriott 10 miles north of Memorial Stadium. Few major-leaguers stay at the team hotel, opting instead for condominiums on the beach or close to one of the many world-class golf courses found in the area.

For Wade, that lifestyle inched closer to reality with his performance in 1993. After accomplishing little in two years at the lowest minor-league level, rookie ball, the tall left-hander thoroughly dominated three loops. Packing a 94-mile-per-hour fastball, Wade overpowered Macon's opponents in the South Atlantic League, breezed through the Carolina League in Durham, then overcame a rough initial outing to handle the Southern League with Greenville. By season's end, he had won 12 of 16 decisions and fanned 208 batters in 158.1 innings, the second-best total in the minors.

Though laudable, that type of performance alone did not merit a major-league job. And when the emerging young pitcher arrived in Florida 20 pounds overweight, thereby affecting his throwing mechanics, he ensured himself an early trip back to the Ramada.

"I just got a minor thing I need to work out, mechanics-wise," Wade said after his final less-than-stunning spring performance. "It's just something that every pitcher goes through, trying to overpower themselves.

"But this has been fun. Their practice is so smooth up here. It's like they don't make mistakes. But it's no different than minor-league camp. You still work your hide off and everything. You just dress in a different place, and you work with the major-league coaches. It's still the same game."

The departure of Wade and the other minor-leaguers protected on the 40-man roster in mid-March left 30 players competing for 25 major-league jobs. Twenty-two of the spots were secured by returning veterans and promising rookies, leaving two availabilities on the 11-man pitching staff and one on the bench, reserved for an outfielder.

Four candidates vied for the two pitching slots. Thirty-four-year-old Mike Bielecki was a Brave in 1992 who has since pitched for two organizations while recovering from reconstructive arm surgery. Thirty-three-year-old Mike Birkbeck was once a prospect in the Milwaukee farm system who pitched the previous year for Atlanta's Triple-A team in Richmond. Milt Hill, 28 and an Atlanta native, was picked off the waiver wire from Cincinnati at the end of the 1993 season. And Gregg Olson, one of the American League's premier closers for the past five years, was but a mere image of his former self because of an ailing elbow he refused to place on the operating table.

The combatants for the final starting outfield spot narrowed to rookies Mike Kelly, Tony Tarasco, Chipper Jones and Ryan Klesko, and newcomer Jarvis Brown, the only flycatcher with any substantial major-league experience. The veteran and four rookies were having exceptional springs, making the decision that much more difficult for Bobby Cox and his staff.

Cox's decision was eased when Black Friday struck the Atlanta camp on the evening of March 16. During an exhibition contest with the New York Yankees in Fort Lauderdale, the skipper witnessed the competition at both pitcher and left field crumble by one. Jones was the first causality when he shredded the anterior cruciate ligament in his right knee while trying to beat out an infield grounder. Later in the game, Olson walked off the mound while pointing to his elbow. Something had popped; the prognosis was not encouraging.

With Olson's status further muddled, the three remaining twirlers readied themselves for the final two weeks. None had pitched significantly better or worse than his competitors, meaning the decision might come down to preferences as much as performances.

Engaged in his 12th spring training, Mike Birkbeck was all too familiar with the factors that take place in deciding who earns a major-league job and who does not. As a promising right-hander climbing the Milwaukee organizational ladder in the mid-1980s, Birkbeck had managers in three separate leagues rate his curveball best among all circuit hurlers. His fastball, on the other hand, was more often compared to the speed of rush-hour traffic. It was for that reason the pitcher's name was usually omitted from top prospect lists.

Even so, it had been more than six years since Birkbeck appeared on any list forecasting success. In between his days as a rising starter with the Brewers and his current status as a journeyman trying to earn a spot on the league's best staff, the Ohio native experienced enough emotional highs and lows to warrant schizophrenia. Amazingly, Birkbeck appears in complete control.

"I suppose I've seen the ups and downs baseball has to offer," Birkbeck said. "The way I look at it, baseball is what I do; it's not who I am. I've struggled. But if the struggles I've experienced in baseball are the worst struggles I'll ever go through in my life, I'll consider myself very lucky.

"I'd like to think I've seen everything. I've been signed, promoted, demoted, outrighted, assigned, optioned, been hurt, been healthy, had success, stunk at times. But a lot of times you just keep playing to see what's going to happen next. I know that I can deal with anything that comes up in this game."

Wiry and unimposing even at 6-foot-2 and 185 pounds, Birkbeck is both nonchalant and profound with his comments. Though the ample pinch of Skoal, now considered contraband in the minors, stuffed between his cheek and gum is typical of most major-leaguers, the words and insight emitting from Birkbeck's mouth are anything but commonplace.

"Physically, I feel as good at this point as I've felt in the last five or six off-seasons," Birkbeck said, the corners of his mouth blackening with the tobacco's juice. "I had some injury problems in '90 that carried over into '91, which caused me to alter my mechanics. That took a lot out of me physically, and I got into some bad habits. Now that those habits are mechanically back to the way I need them to be, my body feels a whole lot better, and my arm feels just wonderful."

The reconstructed mechanics took pressure off Birkbeck's arm, allowing him to repossess his best toss. Because of the strain it puts on a pitcher's arm, exceptional curveballs like the veteran right-hander's are often ostracized and praised only in cases of remarkable movement. Former Brooklyn Dodger manager Charlie Dressen called the pitch, "Public enemy number one. It does nothing but shorten careers."

Birkbeck would have agreed with that assessment a few years earlier. Following an All-American career at Akron University, he joined the Brewers as their fourth-round draft pick in 1983, and a year later was the most accomplished starting pitcher in the Midwest League. He posted a 14-3 record and an earned run average of 2.18 on his way to attaining league all-star honors. His skipper in Beloit, Tom Gomboa, assessed Birkbeck's season thusly, "He has an exceptional big-league curve, and he's improved his command. You can't find a better competitor. He'll find a way to win."

Birkbeck jumped to Double-A El Paso in 1985 and earned all-star recognition while splitting 18 decisions. A promotion to Triple-A Vancouver followed the next season, leading to a 12-6 record and a late-season cup of coffee in Milwaukee, where he was 1-1 in seven outings.

Like many veterans at the Triple A level, Mike Birkbeck was searching for one more shot in the Show. (Photo courtesy of Richmond Braves)

With no pitcher in the Brewer system progressing as smoothly or as rapidly as Birkbeck had over the previous four years, Milwaukee pegged the right-hander for its starting rotation in 1987. He earned the job in spring training before tendinitis in his throwing shoulder cut his season short after 10 starts. He rebounded to go 10-8 in a career-high 23 major-league openings in 1988 only to have shoulder problems shelve him again, this time in September.

The 1989 campaign offered more of the same. Despite an 0-2 record, Birkbeck pitched well in six early-season starts until a weakened right rotator cuff sidelined him for nearly three months. He returned briefly that season to pitch in both the majors and Triple-A, then saw only the minors with Denver in 1990, recording an unimpressive 3-8 mark.

Two weeks after the 1990 major-league campaign concluded, Birkbeck found himself without a job. A broken thumb landed the pitcher under the knife, which led to a knee injury that also required surgery. With his 30th birthday a few months away, Birkbeck encountered few potential employers wanting to hire an aging, banged-up, curveball-throwing pitcher.

"I had a hard time finding a job. I was basically out of the game," said Birkbeck, his marble brown eyes revealing those days were nothing short of trying. "The year before, I'm competing to make a major-league club. The very next, 1991, I'm in minor-league camp with no contract. Fortunately, the Indians let me pitch on their Double-A club, in Canton, which is where I live. First month, I basically did nothing. Then an injury occurred and I got a chance to pitch. I just tried to keep playing and do what I had to do."

After pitching in relief for the first time in his career, Birkbeck threw well enough over the remainder of the season to entice the New York Mets to sign him the following January. He wound up spending the 1992 campaign at Triple-

A Tidewater, going 4-10, even though he allowed less than a hit per inning. He also reappeared in the majors, starting the afterpiece of a doubleheader on August 31, when the Mets were temporarily short on arms.

At season's end, Birkbeck was again a six-year minor-league free agent, and after considering a handful of offers, decided to accept a job hurling for Atlanta's Triple-A club in Richmond. With his health continuing to improve, Birkbeck displayed flashes of his younger self, tying for the International League lead with 13 wins and 136 strikeouts. He was second on the circuit with a 3.11 ERA, and was named the team's most outstanding pitcher.

The revitalized hurler received another boost when Atlanta protected Birkbeck on the team's 40-man roster, thereby giving him a shot at making the major-league club in spring training. And with the Braves trimming their payroll by releasing some high-priced veterans, two openings in long relief are available.

"To be honest, I was really looking forward to the off-season and the potential of being a free agent again," Birkbeck said. "You talk to various people and I know there would have been other good opportunities. Pitching is at a premium right now. When the Braves protected me, initially you think that limits your chances. Now it looks like I have a great opportunity, and I'm very thankful for it."

While Birkbeck's chances of opening the season in Atlanta appeared viable, most observers gave Bielecki little shot of making the team. That was before Bielecki's surgery-scarred arm appeared to be healthy during the first few weeks of March. Bielecki also had the advantage of being a known commodity. Baseball has always thrived on the "old boy network," and toward the end of spring training, it became readily apparent who the leading candidates were simply by the time Atlanta pitching coach Leo Mazzone spent with certain hurlers.

The competition continued through March 28 with the pitchers seemingly entering the day's contest against Montreal in West Palm Beach in a dead-heat. That afternoon, Birkbeck appeared to inch ahead of the others with four innings of solid work and by winning his second game of the spring against no defeats. His stats were also better than those of both Bielecki and Hill, with Birkbeck holding opponents to a .157 batting average, bettering Bielecki (.164) and Hill (.224). Birkbeck and Hill both owned a 2.40 ERA, topping Bielecki's 2.65.

The next morning, those stats meant little after the Braves brass made its decisions. Brown lost out to Kelly, Klesko and Tarasco in the outfield battle. Shortly thereafter, the message came that Cox wanted to see Birkbeck in the manager's office. The right-hander's facial expression changed little upon entering the small office, where Birkbeck was informed that his services were not needed in Atlanta. He had been placed on waivers.

Less than two minutes later, Birkbeck was back at his locker, gathering his belongings. No outburst, no rage, Birkbeck was, as always, in complete control. Nevertheless, when asked a question, his narrow jaw opened, the words struggled to escape.

"Do I think I had any chance?" asked Birkbeck, parroting the inquiry. "I don't think there was a job for me to win. I don't think they think I can pitch in the major leagues."

The other 27 teams over the next two days allowed Birkbeck to pass through waivers. On March 31, Birkbeck agreed to return to Richmond, to keep his dream of returning to the majors alive, and to once again serve as an insurance policy for Atlanta's major-league club.

"I really don't think I did anything that would've prohibited me from making the club," said Birkbeck, who now donned a blue and red cap with a cursive 'R' instead of an 'A'. "The bottom line is, honestly, I didn't throw the ball as well as I could. That's what was so stunning. I was here to make the club, but I didn't put a lot of pressure or emphasis on that. I'll go to Richmond and be ready to make a contribution. They need a support-type player in the organization, and I feel at some point this year I will make a contribution to what they're trying to do in Atlanta, which is win the World Series.

"I have a tremendous amount of confidence in myself, and I've been through a lot in my career. There's a lot of faith and a lot of peace and content wherever I am. I won't necessarily be complacent, but I'll be content just doing my job. As a person, that's all you can do."

Richmond's season was eight days away, and everything seemed to point to Birkbeck taking The Diamond's mound on Opening Day against Toledo.

"I will help Atlanta at some point this season," Birkbeck added. "It's a long year, and a lot of things happen."

2

The City of Monuments

Mike Birkbeck knew that there were worse places in the minors to be headed than Richmond. He had worn the name of nine cities across his chest and visited nearly 100 others across the country. Considering all those times and places, the 1993 campaign, which he spent in the Virginia capital, had been one of the pitcher's more enjoyable seasons of his 11-year career.

"The only thing that makes all this bearable is that I really enjoy Richmond," Birkbeck sighed in between workouts on the day prior to the season's first game. "The ballpark, the way the staff and the fans treat you, it's totally first-class. I know other times in my career that I went places...let's just say it was tough. The situation here, that makes it so much better."

Bruce Baldwin, Richmond's general manager, has been one of the leading and most productive executives during the minors' resurgence over the past decade. A veteran of 22 seasons of baseball operations, Baldwin runs a clean, efficient, family-oriented and award-winning business. Among the unique programs instituted by Baldwin include having employees maintain the same area of the ballpark's exterior grounds on a daily basis as well as bidding patrons "good night" upon exiting the stadium at the game's conclusion.

The general manager's pride in stadium operations stems from the fact that Baldwin was as responsible as anyone in overseeing the building of The Diamond. Erected in an incredible 226 days at a cost of $8 million on the same site of its predecessor, Parker Field, The Diamond was so tagged because of an anonymous letter that suggested during a community drive to name the stadium that the ballpark could become "the diamond of the community."

And the name is fitting. In near-unprecedented cooperation, the City of Richmond and its two neighboring counties, Chesterfield and Henrico, teamed to appropriate $4 million toward the stadium. The remaining moneys were accrued through luxury box leases and donations from the private and public sectors, who rallied around the fund-raising campaign by purchasing 10-dollar buttons that read, "I'm Pitching In To Build A New Ballpark."

Such cooperation spoke volumes on what the game means to the "City of Monuments." Richmond baseball, much like the city itself, drips of history. Dating to 1884, less than two decades after serving as the capital of the Confederacy, Richmond welcomed professional baseball as a charter member of the International League. From there, the hometown team competed in the American Association and the Eastern, Virginia, Atlantic, Virginia-Carolina and Piedmont leagues prior to rejoining the International loop for good in 1954. Nicknames along the way included the Virginians, Giants, Crows, Bluebirds, Johnnie Rebs, Lawmakers and Colts.

Yet, it was not until 1966, following a one-year separation, that professional baseball became stable in Richmond. With the Braves moving their major-league operations from Milwaukee to Atlanta, Richmond was the benefactor, receiving the organization's Triple-A affiliate, formerly the Atlanta Crackers. For the past 28 years, a time when it has been fashionable for major-league teams to show minor-league cities the loyalty of a stray cat by jumping from one locale to another, Richmond and the Braves have enjoyed a marriage that has outlasted all but three current working agreements.

"It's called consistency," Baldwin said. "It helps when kids grow up with the Richmond Braves and now have their own kids. That's one of the most ideal situations you could ever ask for. That enables fans to pass Braves baseball from one generation to the next."

Celebrating its 10th anniversary during the 1994 season, The Diamond has proven to be a trailblazer in the minor leagues. The state-of-the-art complex has seen its plans become the foundation for similar efforts in Charlotte, Ottawa and Norfolk. Among the amenities are 15 leased luxury boxes, a 150-seat restaurant located at club level and spacious clubhouses.

"It's a nice place," Baldwin understated. "We didn't have anything in particular to go by. We just pieced together some things that we thought would work. I think this place has held up well."

Located just north of the intersection of Interstates 64 and 95, The Diamond emerges over the horizon while traveling north. Fans are greeted by Connecticut, a 10-foot by 25-foot sculpture located atop an upper-level concession stand, made to depict an American Indian climbing over a parapet. As for the stands, limited foul territory and a steep slope among the 12,134 seats create a feeling of being both close and on top of the action for all paying customers.

Fans also feel as if they can bond with the players due to the community involvement Baldwin arranges. Every Sunday, a pair of R-Braves sign autographs on the concourse. Public appearances throughout the season also enable community members to shake hands with the city's newest temporary residents.

"We try to treat the players as if they were in the major leagues," Baldwin said. "We respect them and try to realize that we may need their help. There are several public appearances a year. They may bitch and complain a little bit, but it's not bad. It all ties together. If the guys are out in the community, putting out a good image because we're treating them in a professional way, the fans are going to keep coming out. Everything we do the right way can produce better results."

In recent years, the vast majority of players at Richmond and the 27 other Triple-A cities across the country have represented two distinct groups. One involves the young player, the would-be major-leaguer climbing the organizational ladder. The Triple-A level is his last proving ground prior to fulfilling a dream and making the final jump to the Show.

The other and far more common group consists of aging players who for one reason or another do not have the total package to play at the game's top level. Many have tasted life in the Show before a few poor outings, an injury or a difficult situation knocked them back. They acquired a label in the process, which has stuck for the remainder of their playing days, regardless of what they may accomplish in leagues such as the International.

A rare exception to the Triple-A norm took place in Richmond in 1993. Because of the tremendous ripening crop of talent in the Atlanta farm system, the R-Braves fielded a starting lineup that featured a major-league prospect at every position, and was dubbed "The Grady Bunch" by *Baseball America*. Regardless of all the talent, manager Grady Little had his hands full. Little, who skippered Durham and Greenville during the 1991 and 1992 seasons, respectively, had coached most of the players for the previous two years. But it was not long before dissension governed the Richmond clubhouse.

A couple of the heralded players, most notably Ryan Klesko, were not happy about spending another season in the minors. A handful of jealous veterans also created disturbances. The ringleader was Jerry Willard, a 33-year-old catcher, unaffectionately referred to by Little as "that fat f---," who was constantly starting rumors about and picking fights with the prospects. Little swore he would not manage Richmond in 1994 if Willard was re-signed. Fortunately for the Braves, the out-of-shape troublemaker was let go at the end of the year.

The talent wound up shining through despite the various internal problems. After opening the season by losing 11 of their first 18 games, the R-Braves captured first place by the end of June before cruising to a bridesmaid finish and qualifying for the playoffs. Most of the credit was given to the prospects, even though Little was the mastermind behind the success.

Suffice it to say that Little has learned more during his 14 seasons managing in the minors than he lets on. His laid-back style and Texas drawl with a pinch of Cajun can overwhelm his craftiness in managing a game and dealing with his players. He is patient with youngsters, opting for positive reinforcement over intimidation. At the same time, his fuse is typically short with older players. Little isn't above exploding at a veteran if the situation demands it. The balance is delicate, yet Little has managed to discover the right support.

"I just think I've been a fortunate person to have been at the right place at the right time," said Little in his typical self-depreciating manner. "I think I'm just like any other manager at any other level. If the players and the talent are there, they make the manager look good. And the last few years, I've looked awfully good."

Little, similar to most managers in professional baseball, was once in the same shoes as his players. A 12th-round draft pick of the Braves after graduating from Garinger High School in Charlotte, North Carolina, in 1968, Little caught only 75 games in three years with the Atlanta organization due to his being summoned by the U.S. Marine Reserves in 1969. Midway through the 1971 campaign, he joined the Yankees' farm system, where he served as a player/coach for 2½ seasons before focusing solely on the coaching aspects at the Double-A level in 1974.

Just as Little's coaching career seemed to be gaining steam, he suddenly tired of the lifestyle the lower minors offer its participants. He decided to go to central Texas and farm cotton, and for the next five years his only ties to baseball came as a volunteer assistant coach at Texas A&M. By 1979, the long, brutal days in the melting sun and choking dust began to glamorize life in the minors. Little wanted back in the only other profession he knew. He received his chance with the Baltimore Orioles.

"I was very fortunate to get my foot back in the door with the Orioles at that time," said Little, who managed five years in the Baltimore organization and one in the Toronto farm system before joining the Braves as skipper of rookie-level Pulaski in 1986. "I feel like I've progressed along nicely, and I feel like my day will come at the major-league level. I just have to keep going about my business and wait my turn. It will happen. Then all these sacrifices my wife and family have made up to this point in the minor leagues will be repaid."

The 1994 season offered a different challenge for the 44-year-old skipper. The Atlanta roster sported 10 players who served time at Richmond in 1993. That left Little with a more typical Triple-A team. Seventeen of the 22 players had experience at the Class AAA level, and seven of those had at least a cup of coffee in the majors. Nearly every player was fighting long odds to serve as an emergency replacement in the majors, with hopes of quickly proving their worth once they received a shot.

Included in the Richmond fold in 1994 was Terry Clark, a 33-year-old reliever who entered the season with the most minor-league wins, 102, of any active pitcher. Joining Birkbeck in the starting rotation was Mike Hostetler, Brian Bark and Brad Woodall. Mike Potts, Anthony Telford and Pedro Borbon, son of the former Cincinnati pitcher by the same name, are among those toiling in the bullpen.

In the field, Richmond featured a pair of run-through-a-brick-wall players in shortstop Mike Mordecai and outfielder Brian Kowitz. Both players scratched and clawed their way to the top of the minors, refusing to let the indifference shown by the Atlanta brass deter their dreams of playing in the majors. New to the Braves were a pair of players who toiled in 1993 for Charlotte, the defending International League champion. First baseman Luis Lopez, who entered the season with the fourth-best career batting average, .304, among minor-leaguers with at least 2,000 at bats, and right fielder Beau Allred had reached the majors with Los Angeles and Cleveland, respectively. After recovering from career-threatening injuries, both looked to prove themselves in a new organization.

Combine the components and the expectations were not lofty for this makeshift Richmond club. Little, nevertheless, longed to see what the season would bring.

"I feel with this team that you're able to do your job a little bit better," Little said. "Last year we had a large number of players that needed a lot of attention, so we were probably spread a little bit thin in certain areas with certain players. This year we've got some people who need that attention and they're getting a little bit more. That comes from having a few more veterans on the club that know what they're doing. They know what their roles are, they know the things they're trying to improve on. It's just easier when you can give the people that need attention the amount they need."

Two members of the team wound up needing a different type of attention in the minutes leading up to the season opener. First-base coach Tack Wilson was beaned by a line drive on the right side of the head during batting practice. He was taken to the hospital prior to being given medical clearance and released. After realizing he would survive, the good-natured Wilson became the target of countless jokes, if not more baseballs, for the remainder of the season.

Wilson was not the only one needing assistance. Making his final preparations in the trainer's room 45 minutes before game time, Birkbeck cut his right thumb while shaving a callous off his foot. The blade came out of the razor, and he pushed it back in place with the thumb of his pitching hand, creating a one-inch slit. "There was so much blood, it looked like a *Friday the Thirteenth* movie," Birkbeck said.

Since pitchers are not allowed to wear anything on their throwing hand for fear they may create an unfair advantage by scuffing the ball, Birkbeck took the mound without a bandage to protect the cut. Blood continued to ooze from the wound until the second inning. "Once I got some dirt and resin in it and it stopped bleeding, I could throw just about all my pitches," Birkbeck said.

With his typical bulldog tenacity, Birkbeck proceeded to fulfill his duty. Even without the use of a solid breaking ball, the right-hander fanned six Mud Hen batters, scattered five hits and a walk, and did not allow a run over five innings on the first afternoon of the season. The bullpen held the lead in the 7-1 Richmond victory, giving Birkbeck the kind of start he wanted.

"I felt pretty good out there," said Birkbeck, an ice bag taped to an arm that seemed to improve with age. "There were a few pitches I'd like to have back, but for the first game of the year, I'm pleased. If I pitch like that every time out, it might turn out to be a decent season."

Gillis' Greenville

3

Seven hours south of Richmond, the Greenville Braves hoped to equal the Opening Day performance of their Triple-A brethren. After several days of shivery spring showers, the skies cleared to a sea of blue, and combined with a field of green and a clear, crisp breeze, provided a near-perfect setting to begin the Southern League season.

"If you can't get up for today, you've got a chemical imbalance," infielder Doug Wollenburg told anyone who would listen during batting practice.

Directly behind the black net and padded-steel batting cage stood Greenville manager Bruce Benedict, his hands shoved in his back pants pockets, singing lyrics to the country music wailing over the public address system. A former all-star catcher and a 12-year veteran with the Braves, the 38-year-old "Benny" has emerged as the golden child among minor-league managers in the Atlanta farm system. Though Bobby Cox's job in the majors is secure, a successor must be groomed. Benedict is the chosen one, the man on the corporate fast track.

Benedict has been associated with the Atlanta organization since the Braves drafted him in the fifth round in 1976. When he hung up the tools of ignorance for the final time in 1988, he began serving as a roving catching instructor. His most impressive efforts came in his diligent and patient work with Javy Lopez, which enabled the young Dominican to blossom from a raw, talented prospect into a major-league caliber catcher. The Atlanta front office took notice and asked Benedict if he would like to manage the rookie-level Danville Braves in 1993.

Wanting to see what he could accomplish at the dugout helm, Benedict guided Danville to a 38-30 mark in the short-season Appalachian League. That showing brought an unexpected promotion to Greenville, one that surprised many people within the organization. Rarely does one land the head job in Double-A with just a half-season of managing experience. However, given his knowledge of the game, his major-league background and the leadership ability acquired from his days behind the plate, Benedict was deemed worthy, even at the expense of others.

The Braves were well aware that Benedict would be challenged at Greenville in 1994. For that reason, the organization armed him with a coaching staff that would undoubtedly make the callow manager look good. Pitching coach Bruce Dal Canton headed a young and talented staff after tutoring Richmond's hurlers for the past three years, while Randy Ingle, who managed Class A Macon in 1993 and may be the most popular coach in the organization, served as the G-Braves' hitting instructor. Brian Snitker, another former manager at Macon, was an extra authority figure until Danville's season began in mid-June, when he becomes the rookie team's hitting coach.

"I'm looking forward to this season and the challenges it brings," Benedict said. "Managing at this level is going to be different for me compared to last season. But I love this time of year, and I love working for this organization. That's very rare, to work 19 years with the same organization like I have. We're at the pinnacle of the profession right now. Our minor-league system over the last couple of years has been very successful. The smile can't get any bigger than when I start talking about Braves baseball."

Before Benedict completed his final sentence, the music on the public address system came to an abrupt halt. A few moments of silence followed until a loud roaring hiss that resembled the Atlantic Ocean began to emit from the stadium's speakers. A fuse had blown less than an hour prior to game time, thereby giving Greenville general manager Steve DeSalvo yet another hurdle to clear before the on-field announcements take place before the first pitch.

Other minor events revealed that it was Opening Night. The press box food from a local barbecue restaurant did not arrive on time, further stressing first-year public relations director Matt Garvey, who was already steaming over the absence of the team's press guide. Add a crisis or two at one of the concession stands, along with some miscommunications between other front-office personnel, and the arrangements started to take form as one tremendous snafu.

An hour later, thanks to some fast phone calls, faster orders and even faster footwork by DeSalvo, everything fell into place. Nary any of the 3,000 or so fans who visited Greenville Municipal Stadium on that early April evening had even the slightest hint of any chaos. As far as they were concerned, it was business as usual. Fans were being greeted, the concessions were flowing and baseball commenced for the 11th straight season off Mauldin Road.

Greenville, at one time a large factory town that has emerged as a magnet for young professionals over the past dozen years, joins the rest of the region in loving its high school and college football. Baseball, meanwhile, has typically been an activity between the conclusion of spring football practice and the opening of preseason drills in August. Other than the past few years, when the Atlanta Braves have kept the fans' interest in the sport well into the month of October, the city's long-term attraction toward the summer game has been mild at best.

Professional baseball in Greenville dates to 1907, when the Mountaineers climbed the standings for one year in the South Carolina League before folding at the end of the season. A year later, the Spinners began a four-season stint in the Carolina Baseball Association before the city competed four separate times, covering 24 years, in the South Atlantic League, one season in the Palmetto and four campaigns in the Tri-State.

In 1963, Greenville opened a 10-year tour in the Class A Western Carolinas League, always taking the name of its major-league affiliate, including Braves, Mets, Red Sox and Rangers. That lasted through 1972, when Meadowbrook Park smoldered as so many ashes after a small fire built to an inferno with the help of the ballpark's rotting wood structure.

Greenville was without professional baseball for 11 years until a group of civic leaders and businessmen convinced Braves officials to move the team's Double-A operations from aging Grayson Stadium in Savannah, Georgia, to a spanking new facility in South Carolina for the 1984 season. Since that time, Greenville has established itself as one of the top franchises at the Class AA level. The G-Braves have posted the Southern League's best record, and are one of only two Double-A franchises to draw more than 200,000 fans for the past 10 seasons, the best of those years being 1992 with 253,229 patrons.

According to DeSalvo, about 15 to 20 percent of the G-Braves' fans keep abreast of the action on a daily basis. "The rest are people who are looking for a fun night out and some family entertainment," DeSalvo said. "They're looking for something that's safe, respectable and reasonably priced. I think we're able to give that to them as well as anyone else."

It would not be wrong to say that Greenville Municipal Stadium is a place to be seen, especially among the younger sect. Teen-agers constantly walk from one end of the concourse to the other in the amphitheater-style setting, caring little about what takes place on the field below. The few times the preening teens realize that baseball is being played occurs when a frequent foul ball and the subsequent mad dash for the white sphere interferes with their wandering paths.

The facility itself is comfortable, seating a hair more than 7,000 fans in a combination of red and blue chair-back seats and aluminum benches. Bruce Baldwin, Richmond's current general manager and the Southern League's executive of the year in 1984, cut his teeth by overseeing construction of Greenville's ballpark before heading north. About the only complaints ever heard regarding the stadium concern the lack of a covering for the fans. Budgetary limitations forced the townspeople in 1983 to vote for a paved parking lot over protection from the elements. The open-air setting has led the team to schedule every game at 7:15 in the evening, for the midsummer heat is fierce enough to frighten even the most religious sun worshippers.

The other groans come from the crowd's elitists. Those viewing the game from the press box or one of the two luxury boxes must leave their perch and go downstairs when nature calls. Nearly every time Henry Aaron had to make the trip during his stint as the Braves' farm director, he would announce sarcastically, "It's time to venture into the land of the great unwashed." G-Braves play-by-play broadcaster Mark "Doogie" Hauser admits that during his first three years with the team, he filled more than one empty two-liter bottle of Pepsi while on the air.

Nevertheless, most everyone at Greenville Municipal Stadium was content and excited about the opening of a new season. That especially held true for the G-Braves players. Anchoring the club is a starting rotation that features former Florida State outfielder Chris Brock and four 21-year-old pitching prospects — Terrell Wade, Jason Schmidt, Chris Seelbach and Jerry Koller. Brad Clontz and Tom Thobe are slated to receive the majority of save opportunities in relief.

Atypical of the Double-A level, where rosters typically feature more prospects from top to bottom than any other level in the minors, Greenville fielded a more veteran lineup, including three returning players from the 1993 club in the infield and two more in the garden. Newcomer Tony Graffanino, a self-assured second baseman who emerged as a prospect at Durham in 1993, joined first baseman Tim Gillis, third sacker Ed Giovanola and shortstop Hector Roa. The outfield included returnees Kevin O'Connor and Pedro Swann playing with the promoted Don Robinson and Miguel Correa.

"The start of the year is always a lot of fun," Tim Gillis said after batting practice. "Every year you come out of spring training, you always think this is going to be your biggest year. Hopefully it'll happen for me."

One of the most consistent players for Greenville in 1993, Gillis hit .251 while leading the team with 62 runs batted in and 14 home runs. His reddish-brown hair, long face and Southern accent epitomize his friendly "aw shucks" personality. Yet, on the field, the corner infielder is as competitive as anyone, doing whatever it takes to make his dream of climbing the ladder to the game's top level become reality.

Though excited about starting another year, Gillis opened the 1994 campaign standing on the same rung as the previous season. The Braves admitted that Gillis could be playing and succeeding at the Triple-A level. Instead, the

Atlanta brass determined the Greenville roster needed veteran leadership, a player who could keep the team together with his solid example when the turbulent moments struck. No one ever sat down with Gillis and told him that role was expected. The Atlanta front office knew the formality was unnecessary.

"I think I'm a guy my teammates look up to a little bit," Gillis admitted. "Hopefully I can help some of them play in the big leagues. This game's not just about one person. Every year's a new year. You can make it as good as you want it to be. If you're playing on a bad team, it's going to make your year bad, no matter how good you do individually. You got to go out and be a team player first and let everything else take care of itself.

A leader of men, Tim Gillis took one for the organization by returning to Greenville instead of being promoted to Richmond. (Photo courtesty of Greenville Braves)

"At the same time, I'm a little disappointed about coming back here. Every year you go out, you want to progress. I was a little upset, but I think everybody is when they have to repeat a level after they feel they've done the job to get to the next level. It's happened before to other people and it's happened to me. I know how to handle it. I'm not going to draw up and be mad the whole year. That's just going to put you in a hole. You just got to roll with the punches and see what happens."

Gillis is in many ways a survivor. No one expected him to advance to the Double-A level. Every major-league club told him that much during the 1989 amateur draft. A record 1,490 players were selected during the three-day affair, but Gillis' name was never called.

"I can't really answer that," said Gillis after being asked why he felt he was bypassed after a solid four-year career at Livingstone University. "There were a few scouts looking. I guess they just didn't see what they liked. I believed I could play. There's a lot of people that thought I could play and there's a lot of people that thought I couldn't play. It makes it a little bit sweeter when you come out, you work hard, you get an opportunity and you show everybody and yourself that you can do the job."

Refusing to abandon hope following the draft, Gillis played in a college league during the summer of 1989, then completed his management science degree in computer engineering and worked out with the Livingstone team in the fall. His determination finally reaped rewards one day in October when Atlanta scout Dickie Martin came to see one of Livingstone's pitchers.

"I went over and talked to him," Gillis said. "I had a couple of tryout invitations lined up, and I was hoping to get a tryout with him. Basically, I just told him that I could play and that I wanted to play."

His sales pitch successful, Gillis showed enough defensive versatility and offensive competency to convince Martin and the Braves to ink the Crestview, Florida, native to a standard contract on October 28, 1989. He had been presented a place on the ladder; it was Gillis' responsibility to climb it.

"I remember standing out in the outfield a few months later in spring training, just shagging fly balls my first day," said Gillis, his eyes lighting up in remembrance of the moment. "I was in awe, seeing everybody wearing 'Braves' across their chest. It was a huge thrill. I'll never forget that. It doesn't seem like that long ago, but it's been four years. It probably didn't mean a lot to most other people, but to me, it was like, 'I can't believe I'm finally here.'"

Gillis immediately established himself. At Class A Burlington he batted .256 with a dozen roundtrippers and 61 RBIs. His play at the hot corner was stellar enough to earn recognition as the organization's best defensive player at the position. He was promoted to Durham in 1991, but after hitting .246, he returned to Durham Athletic Park a year later. The stall was temporary, for Gillis swatted 21 long balls, fourth-best in the Carolina League, before landing a late-season promotion to Greenville, where he stayed the entire 1993 campaign.

While reaching the Double-A level is a feat the majority of signed players never obtain, Gillis is aware of his situation. Not only had his career stalled once again in 1994, his baseball clock continued to tick. He entered the season at 26 years old, an age when many players are beginning to establish themselves in the majors. If he was going to fulfill his dream, Gillis realized time was beginning to work against him.

"You think about it in the back of your mind," Gillis said. "Every day you're getting a little older. Every day you're not in the big leagues, it seems like the older you get and the farther away you get from the big leagues in terms of what upper level management thinks. Everybody nowadays wants to see the young phenom come up at 22 years old and take the world by storm. Me, I just got to be ready whenever the time arises."

Such moments of reflection cause Gillis' mind to search for the positive. He, along with every other minor-league player in his situation, had found two sources of inspiration over the past year. Bill Taylor, a relief pitcher who was in the Atlanta organization in 1993, received his first taste of the major leagues at age 34. Infielder Rich Amaral was a rookie with the Seattle Mariners in 1993 even though his birth certificate revealed he was 31. If they could make it, Gillis surmised, so too could he.

"Those guys were persistent, and I'm sure there were times along the way they were thinking, 'Man, somebody must not think I can play,'" Gillis said. "That's a lot of sacrifices they and their families had to make. It makes it a lot sweeter. Guys like myself look at that. I'll probably appreciate it more than the common fan because I'm going through the same thing.

"It just takes one big year at this level. That's the way I look at it. And if you got a job coming out of spring training, you still got a chance to make it to the big leagues. That's the only reason I play the game, to play in the big leagues. The thing is, I still don't think I've peaked as a player. Hopefully you peak at the highest level there is. Hopefully this year will take me closer to it."

With his confidence packed and his dreams in tow, Gillis jogged down the right-field line to the cinder-block clubhouse to make his final preparations for the game. A few hours later, Gillis scored once and Graffanino registered the second run in Greenville's 2-1 victory over visiting Knoxville. In what would prove to be a harbinger for the season, G-Braves hitters scratched out just one hit, a 10-foot bouncer that no Smokie fielders could reach in a timely fashion. The pitching, conversely, was superb, with Wade resuming his overpowering ways of the previous campaign before giving way to the bullpen after reaching his early-season pitch limit of 75 tosses.

"I had a little minor problem," Wade reminisced about the spring while rubbing lotion on his hands. "I went back and watched some of my old tapes so that I could get back in the motion like I was last year. I'm on track now.

"As for tonight, I felt stronger as the innings went on. The first start is always the hardest. Once you get that start out of the way, everything seems to fall into place. You don't have to worry about things like pitch counts and that stuff. It was a good start. Everybody worked together. Even though we got just one hit, we scored the runs when we needed to."

Down in Durham

4

Matt Murray harbored no resentment toward Durham, North Carolina. In fact, the 6-foot-6, 235-pound right-handed pitcher had experienced success in the "City of Medicine" during a brief two-game stint early in the 1991 season. He even liked the ballpark, Durham Athletic Park, referred to locally as "The Dap." Many hurlers often include a vulgarity or two in their descriptions, due largely to its short right-field wall.

The truth be known, Murray had absolutely no desire to be in Durham. If he had his druthers, he would have been farther south, in Greenville, pitching for Atlanta's Double-A club. He even had visions of jumping to Richmond during spring training, but deep down he knew that Greenville was a more realistic destination to begin the season.

Those plans, no matter how feasible, changed during the final days of spring training. After starting the spring in major-league camp and displaying solid progress during his minor-league outings, Murray was assigned by the Braves to the Durham roster. That placement left the right-hander as confused as he was upset.

"I don't know what's going on here," Murray said prior to the Bulls' home opener on April 15, after beginning the season with a seven-game swing through Prince William and Lynchburg. "The front office doesn't tell us anything. It's just, 'You're going to Durham.'"

The pitcher was not the only player wondering about his placement in Durham. Catcher Brad Rippelmeyer and pitcher Blase Sparma were back in the Carolina League after spending unsuccessful seasons with Greenville in 1993. Both players knew that their demotions did not bode well for their careers. Repeating a year at the same level is one thing, but to move down a rung on the ladder after a full season at the one above is a more disheartening experience entirely. To make matters worse, other players moved ahead of them on the corporate ladder.

The Braves understood the players' feelings. Chuck LaMar and his managers, coaches and staff went to great lengths in building the teams of every minor-league affiliate during the final days of March in

West Palm Beach. After the major-league roster had been established by John Schuerholz, Bobby Cox and his coaches, LaMar and his assistants determined the remaining lineups in the organization during numerous meetings that essentially uplifted the careers of some players and effectively destroyed any expectations of others. Every player is slotted with a specific role in mind. That allows the manager of each of the four full-season teams to know what the organization expects from everyone in uniform. Certain guys are deemed prospects and need to play every day. Others are pigeon-holed as reserves, requiring them to open some eyes every time they take the field. The youngest players in need of hands-on work are ticketed for extended spring training until the short-season leagues started in mid-June. The remainder are simply handed their walking papers and a one-way ticket home.

Murray's disappointment, unlike those of his teammates, had little historical merit. Despite having pitched in the organization since 1988, the 23-year-old had climbed no higher than Durham. Instead, Murray spent more than half of his six years in the organization nursing a bad elbow and overcoming subsequent surgery. Those events retarded his progress and produced more question marks than answers.

That's not to say that the Braves did not have hopes for the young pitcher. The team grabbed him in the second round of the 1988 draft after most other clubs rated him first-round, but unsignable, material. A top prospect at Loomis Chaffee High School in Windsor, Connecticut, Murray was considered a high-risk pick. He had been admitted to the private high school as a transfer student from his Swampscott, Massachusetts, home on the understanding that he repeat his junior year and remain there for two years. Even so, he was eligible to be drafted since his high school class in Massachusetts graduated, and the Braves came up with the appropriate five figures in his bonus to net his signature.

Murray began his climb in the organization by earning Top 10 prospect recognition in the Appalachian League from *Baseball America* after striking out 76 batters in 54 innings at Pulaski as a 17-year-old in 1988. A year later, he posted a combined 4-5 record at Bradenton and Sumter, then blossomed to an 11-7 mark and tied for second in the Midwest League with three shutouts at Burlington in 1990.

After rapid progress up the organizational ladder, Murray soon found more heartbreak than hope waiting for him in Durham. Pitching on a damp, cool Opening Day evening, he felt something stiffen in his right arm, particularly around the elbow. After picking up the win, he took the ball again four nights later, but was unable to perform one time through the batting order. At the

Matt Murray was determined not to let a serious arm injury and subsequent surgery end his career. (Photo courtesy of Durham Bulls)

team's insistence, Murray flew to Atlanta to meet with the Braves' orthopedic physician, Dr. Joe Chandler.

"The first time I went to see the doctor, I really didn't think it was that serious," Murray said. "I thought it was tendinitis. Then Dr. Chandler said, 'You have a serious problem with your elbow.' I was just blown away. I couldn't believe it. This had never happened to me."

The Braves, Chandler and Murray sat down and considered the two paths that could be traveled at this fork in the pitcher's career. Surgery would require at least a year's worth of rehabilitation. Rest could strengthen the arm without the lingering effects surgery would create. If everything went as hoped, Murray could be back on the mound no later than the start of the 1992 season.

"We decided to rehab it and it looked encouraging," Murray said. "During instructional league that fall, it felt good, but I was still skeptical, and I think so was Dr. Chandler. I kept thinking to myself, 'I'm not out of the woods yet.'

"I came to big league camp and threw the next spring. I knew something was still wrong. I think it was just a matter of time before the elbow completely blew out."

Time, rest and rehabilitation had proven unsuccessful, forcing Murray to take the less-desirable road to recovery. He underwent reconstructive surgery known in the industry as "Tommy John surgery," considered a last-ditch effort to salvage a pitcher's ability. Sometimes a pitcher returns in top form; other times the hurler comes back only a mere image of his former self. Murray realized the uphill battle that awaited him. No longer was he just climbing the organizational ladder; he was also beginning a journey that would prove to be as mentally trying as it was physically demanding.

"I never thought about my career too much until I was lying on the bed in pre-op getting ready to go into the operating room," Murray said. "All the sudden, it was like, 'I'm going to get cut on!' I started thinking, second-guessing myself. Maybe I should have gone to college or done something else. I was 21 at the time. I didn't have any significant college. It was like, 'What do I do now? What can I do other than throw a baseball?'"

The surgery was deemed a success, and Murray, sporting a four-inch scar on his inner elbow, began focusing his efforts on rebuilding the strength needed to throw the stitched sphere up to major-league standards. Countless hours of grievous rehab followed, consuming the remaining nine months of 1992 and the first few weeks of 1993. When he finally climbed a mound in West Palm Beach, Murray felt a rush of adrenaline combined with a thrust of fear.

"When I started throwing in extended spring training, that was the most nervous I've ever been," Murray said. "It's weird, because your arm is doing something you've done a thousand times before, yet your new arm has never really done it at all."

In addition to having a ligament in his elbow replaced with one from his left wrist, the surgery also involved moving the elbow muscles closer together, resulting in a great deal of stiffness and tightness. When he began throwing, Murray had to rest his arm for six days before resuming. Though slow, to Murray's delight, his arm responded with aplomb while his pitching overwhelmed. In 15 starts against South Atlantic League hitters in 1993, Murray won seven of 10 decisions with an incredible earned run average of 1.83.

"After my first win, our pitching coach, Larry Jaster, presented me with a ball that said, 'Matt Murray's first win in two years,'" Murray said. "It was like my first year again. I was totally starting over, and it was a lot of fun. But I also realized I was a different pitcher from what I used to be."

The promise and the potential were still present in the opening stanzas of 1994. Murray realized the Braves had stuck with him through the extended injury longer than most teams would have. He had been on the 40-man roster for nearly three years. That fact helped Murray know that even though he is now in Durham, Atlanta was still interested in what he may be able to accomplish.

"I'm definitely grateful," Murray said. "All my teammates joke with me, asking me what I'm doing to get all this. I just thank God. I don't know why the Braves did it. It's definitely a vote of confidence from them, that they believe in me. And this is the year when I want to really repay them and do well and show them I was worth all the trouble they went through. I mean, two years and I threw seven innings! Seven innings."

To Murray's dismay, his repayments continued with Durham, a team led by manager Matt West, a former minor-league pitcher with the Braves. West served as the Bulls' pitching coach for the past two years and now, at age 34, was receiving his first taste of managing after practically pleading for the job the past couple winters.

"I think this is something I've been meant to do for quite a number of years," West said in his best corporate voice. "Ironically enough, the transition has probably been a little easier for me. When I was a pitching coach, I always had in the back of my mind all of these things that I'd like to do if I was running things. I think it was an inkling I had that I wanted to be a part of the entire program and be in charge of that. So it's kind of like I've been a manager in waiting for three or four years and now I can just be myself."

Exactly who West is can be debated. A graduate of California State University at Long Beach, the former pitcher considers himself an intellectual compared to others in the game, and possesses a sardonic sense of humor that often goes over the head of an unsuspecting young player. He wants desperately for everyone to know who is in charge, usually to the point of being a control freak regarding the routine duties required of a manager. An example of that comes during his pregame preparations. West refuses to abide by the time-honored rituals of many old-school managers, such as shooting the breeze with the opposing skipper, reporters and the team's broadcaster. To interview West, appointments often have to be made in advance. Five minutes is the maximum length, provided something else does not come up.

For the players who understand him, West hung the moon. He does not waste a minute on the field. When players stretch prior to games, West is beside them, getting inside their heads. When players warm up their arms, he observes every movement. "You're opening up too f---ing soon," West instructs. "Let your arm come through your body. Otherwise you'll end up f---ing up your arm and start throwing like a f---ing girl." He's an educator every bit as much as anyone standing in front of a grade school classroom, and damn proud of it.

"I think that anybody at this level and below is a teacher," West said during a scheduled meeting. "The joy of what we do isn't the baby-sitting and the housekeeping and the paperwork; it's the on-the-field elements and actually seeing that gleam in a player's eye when he starts to get what you've been trying to get him to do. Oftentimes if you keep them healthy and keep them motivated and having fun, sending them out there in between the white lines is going to teach them a lot of lessons that verbalizing things are not."

Regardless of his approach, West was saddled with a roster that featured 15 graduates of the 1993 Macon club. Most of the players are gritty, hard-nosed athletes who do not possess the press clippings that many others in the organization sport. Among those are pitcher Mike D'Andrea, a right-hander who parties as intensely as he battles on the mound; second baseman Marty Malloy, a Pete Rose clone who wouldn't give an inch to a crippled grandmother; third baseman Robert Smith, who is on the verge of becoming a top prospect once he puts his above-average tools together; and outfielder Tom Waldrop, a hard-hitting, albeit inconsistent, right fielder who displays flashes of greatness when he's in a zone at the plate.

As far as the heralded ones are concerned, two Bulls are considered to have the horns. Jamie Arnold is a former No. 1 draft pick who is trying to find some harmony with his pitches. And center fielder Damon Hollins, at 19 the youngest player in the Carolina League, had been placed in Durham after playing at rookie-level Danville in 1993. The Braves were challenging the outfielder by allowing him to skip Macon, hoping he will overcome any initial struggles to jump to the head of the fast-track class.

"We had a lot of hopes for this ballclub because there's a tremendous amount of ability here and because I'm a positive person," West said. "Offensively, I think we've been pretty steady in the early going. This league and this level of play is quite a jump for a number of our position players. The old saying about the pitchers being ahead of the hitters certainly applied during that first road trip. But I think we're starting to see those things filter out of their game plan. They're making the adjustments. The prospects for us are very bright."

The final sands apparently fell through the hour glass with that comment. Without a word, West tugged on the bill of his blue Bulls cap, nearly covering his cutting blue eyes, and marched near the first base coach's box. He stood there silently with his legs crossed and his weight shifted toward his right side, leaning on the end of a bat until the opponent's batting practice commenced some three minutes later.

West's apparent lack of social skills with those not wearing a Bulls uniform had not become contagious and didn't afflict Durham general manager Peter Anlyan. If ever a mold for a general manager was deemed necessary, Anlyan would find himself in plaster. Bright, articulate and genuine, Anlyan serves as the new leader for the team's owner, Capital Broadcasting, after working on the company's television side for eight years.

In many ways, Anlyan is the envy of his contemporaries. Thanks to the movie *Bull Durham*, Anlyan heads an operation that sells itself as the quintessential minor-league team. Travelers often drive out of their way to visit and walk around the ballpark, even in the middle of winter. Anlyan realizes the attraction and keeps The Dap's front gate open during the day until final preparations must be made for that evening's contest.

"Folks seem to want to walk in and take a look to see if they see Kevin Costner or Susan Sarandon," Anlyan said. "Just last weekend, there was a guy who played here in '67. He called me ahead of time from Chicago and said, 'I'm coming down to a wedding and I want to bring my son by and take him out to the mound and show him where I pitched.' I could tell that the wedding wasn't quite as important as bringing his son out here to stand on the mound."

The club's popularity created a boom in souvenir sales for the team, with the demand becoming so great that the team operates a gift store across the street from The Dap. Best estimates have the Bulls raking in close to a half-million dollars from the sale of caps, shirts and other novelties sporting the classic snorting bull jumping through the letter "D". Those figures easily make Durham the most popular minor-league club in terms of annual souvenir sales.

The souvenirs and novelties are simply a part of the minor-league experience offered in Durham, which first began hosting professional baseball in 1902 as a charter member of the Class D North Carolina League. Following the game's 11-year absence, Durham competed in the North Carolina State League (1913-1917), the Piedmont League (1920-1933, 1936-1943) and the Carolina League (1945-1967) before sharing a team with Raleigh for four years (1968-1971). Another long baseball-less stretch followed, one lasting eight years, as the advent of air conditioning, nationally televised games and a vast array of additional entertainment activities that afflicted many other minor-league cities in the late 1950s and 1960s struck Durham.

It was not until 1980 that the minors experienced the embryologic stages of a rebirth. Miles Wolff, a local resident and soon-to-be publisher of *Baseball America* magazine, decided to bring the summer game back to Durham by shelling out a franchise fee of $2,500 to the Carolina League. The positive response was almost immediate, with the Bulls attracting an unheard-of 175,963 fans. By comparison, the 1967 season drew 24,000 patrons.

Unlike fans in other minor-league parks, Durham's faithful immediately showed an uncanny appreciation for what was taking place on the field. Featuring an eclectic mix, ranging from tobacco field workers to businessmen to college professors who sat side-by-side in seats that are as close to the action as any in the minors, the ballpark quickly became a favorite on the circuit for the home team and visitors alike.

"It's a great place to play," said Tommy Thompson, who caught and played third base for the Bulls between 1980 and 1982. "They're great fans. When I was here, they cheered for good plays by both teams and enjoyed good baseball. I got close to some Duke law students with an ongoing relationship near third base. They came out, drank heavily and supported us really well."

Annual attendance continued to hover close to 150,000 until *Bull Durham* was released in the summer of 1988. That year more than 272,000 fans clicked through The Dap's turnstiles before the team eclipsed the 300,000 barrier in 1990. Those figures not only surpassed every other Class A team, but also outdrew most Double- and Triple-A franchises as well.

The record-breaking numbers did not transpire without difficulties in other phases of the team's operations. Though nostalgic and inviting, The Dap, built in 1939 and lacking many of the conveniences now required under the Professional Baseball Agreement between the major and minor leagues, was no longer a viable venue for the Bulls. However, the voters of Durham rejected a referendum for a new facility, leaving Wolff with limited opportunities. Frustrated, Wolff finally decided to sell the team for a whopping $3.8 million in 1990 to Jim Goodmon, who headed Capital Broadcasting.

The Durham City Council grasped the seriousness of the situation shortly thereafter, realizing that Durham proper could once again be without baseball, and approved the erection of an $11 million stadium that would replace The Dap in 1994. Because North Carolina laws require three bids before awarding contracts of more than $100,000, the new stadium fell behind schedule after the process needed four tries to receive a trio of estimates. Therefore, The Dap was back in use for the 1994 campaign, its 55th year of existence, even though the team had promoted ad nauseam that the previous season was the final year professional baseball would be played off Morris Street.

"We're having a little fun with 'The Second Annual Final Season at The Dap,'" Anlyan said. "A few reporters have called up and tried to dig out of me that, yeah, everybody is real embarrassed that we're back here. That isn't the case at all. We're fine with being here.

"Who wouldn't want to experience another season here? We never have a special guest sing the national anthem because we have a tradition of singing it ourselves. You have all your regular season-ticket holders under the grandstand. Each bleacher has its own personality. The folks down the third-base line, they're kind of the rowdies, the college kids. The first-base side, they're generally a bit older and not quite as rowdy. It's just great.

"The one thing that struck me when I first took this job is that it reminded me a lot of college basketball. I think one of the reasons that minor-league baseball is so popular around here is there's a certain purity to it. These players are working real hard. They're trying to prove themselves. They're not playing for huge salaries. There's a lot of heart put into the game. I think that has something to do with the appeal of minor-league ball now."

The promise of a new stadium landed the Bulls on the road for the season's first week. Because of an inability to get the hitters and pitchers on the same wavelength on the same nights, Durham opened the campaign with just two wins in its first seven contests. In his season debut, Murray was tagged with the loss in the third game, a 5-0 defeat at Prince William. The Bulls also dropped Murray's second start, a 6-5 result at Lynchburg, although the pitcher had taken a seat in the dugout by the time the game was decided. Those outings, though far from horrendous, did little to alter the pitcher's feelings about life in the Class A city.

"It's hard not to get down on yourself when you know you should be dominating guys at this level and you're not," Murray said. "Things will get better. They got to, or else they'll be shipping me out of town in an ambulance."

Lovable Losers

5

The early-season woes of Matt Murray and the Bulls paled in comparison to what was taking place one step down the organizational ladder in Macon, Georgia. The Braves handed manager Leon Roberts one of the most talented, yet the youngest team on any full-season circuit in the minors. Macon's average age was 20 years and six months, nearly one year below the South Atlantic League average and two full years younger than the loop's oldest club, Savannah. Those numbers reveal Atlanta's approach to developing players. The organization drafts and signs mostly high school athletes who can be molded and groomed to the Braves' way of doing things, instead of older players whose habits must be altered and their potential quickly recaptured after their days on the college diamonds.

Macon's youth was evident during the season-opening series in Charleston, South Carolina. The Braves committed six official errors and at least as many mental miscues in the lidlifter. By the end of the evening, more than 5,000 Charleston fans had seen the home team begin life as the RiverDogs in style, pummeling Macon, 16-1.

The following night, pitcher Carey Paige, a third-round draft pick in 1992, fanned eight Charleston batters and surrendered just four hits before reaching his pitch limit after five innings of work. The Macon hitters, meanwhile, posted a 4-1 lead after seven innings before the RiverDogs rallied to a 6-4 triumph.

That performance, albeit a losing one, enabled Roberts to breathe a little easier prior to the home-opener on Saturday evening, April 9. He understood the challenge he faced. A large man who played 12 years in the major leagues and possesses the patience of Job, Roberts was selected for the trying job of developing raw prospects after a yeoman's effort in 1992 and 1993 at Durham. A younger, less-experienced skipper might suffocate under the pressure of having to lead a club such as Macon, but the 43-year-old Roberts felt at ease and completely in control.

"Sometimes you got to demonstrate a hair more patience and that comes with the territory at this level," Roberts said. "The job is to train potential major-leaguers. A manager has to work hard to stay in their corner and help them out and motivate them and push them and challenge them and pat them on the back and all that stuff. The way I look at it is, I'm going to try to polish them the best way that I know how to set the stage for them to be productive, impact players for the big team in the near future."

The Braves do not mask their goals and objectives at their minor-league venues. Victories and championships are nice, but unquestionably secondary. Instead, the organization wants first and foremost to develop major-league players. If that means promoting a popular and productive player at the expense of the minor-league club and its fans he is leaving behind, so be it. And if it means an excessive number of notches in the loss column for a team, that's fine as long as the proper number of players display individual signs of progress over the course of the season.

That approach has its share of critics. Even though the Braves own the Richmond, Greenville and Macon franchises, thereby relieving any pressure regarding the local team's bottom line, the general managers still have a more difficult time attracting fans if the club's record is abysmal. There are also those in other organizations who believe winning and losing are contagious. Regardless of how well a player may develop individually, they reason, he never reaches his full potential unless he learns how to win by virtue of the team concept.

Atlanta counterbalances those criticisms by operating an organization that focuses on the players. With eight clubs from top to bottom in the farm system, typically one and in some cases two more than most other organizations, the Braves give their players more opportunities to succeed than any team in the game.

"If a player can't make it with the Atlanta organization, he can't make it with anyone," said Chuck LaMar. "I've seen some teams give players little more than a couple of weeks. They'll draft a player in June, watch him in July, and release him at the end of August.

"We give every player at least one spring. That way he can play in the season and in the spring. We won't cut a first-year player unless there are extenuating circumstances. That's why we have three rookie league teams. Idaho Falls is there to see what players we drafted out of college can do against professional pitching. Danville is where we put our advanced high school players. And West Palm, our Gulf Coast League affiliate, is where our young high school players begin. No one gives a borderline player a longer look than the Braves."

Once a player reaches Macon, the organization's first full-season stop on the ladder to the majors, he has had a chance to prove himself at the professional level. And the 1994 Macon team featured some fast climbers. Twelve of the 25 players joined the organization the previous summer, with nine of them uniting via the draft. In fact, except for Paige and pitcher Ryan Jacobs, nearly everyone who is considered a prospect on the team was signed in 1993 and spent the last campaign playing for one of the organization's three short-season teams. Fifth-round pick Del Mathews was a member of the Macon pitching staff, joining fellow prospects shortstop Danny Magee, a sixth-round pick; center fielder Andre King, the Braves' first choice; and 17th-round selection Jermaine Dye, Macon's right fielder.

Playing the game, however, was just one of the challenges that awaited young players in the low minors. Most were away from home for the first time and have never experienced the freedom of living on their own. Professional baseball's working hours are not conducive to a moderate lifestyle for the immature. Players are typically out of the clubhouse well before midnight and do not have to return to the ballpark until two or three the following afternoon. For a young man who feels as if he has just been freed from his cage, trouble can be waiting around the first corner.

One thing that often limits the amount of trouble a player comes across involves a lack of money. Braves players in their first year at Macon receive $1,000 a month during the season, $50 more if it's their second season on the loop. That figure jumps to $1,100 for players in the first season at Durham, $1,300 a month at Greenville, and $1,700 every 30 days at Richmond. Only players with at least one season at the Double-A or Triple-A level have an opportunity to be financially rewarded for outstanding performances. The only other cash coming in is meal money during road trips. Class A players receive $15 a day for food when traveling, a dollar less than Double-A players, and three bills less than the Triple-A per diem.

From those thousand monthly clams, Class A players must find and pay for living arrangements in their new cities. In Macon, as in most other towns, the team puts together a list of apartment complexes and occasionally local families that offer places to rent. Players in the low minors, most of whom are not married, usually join three other teammates and rent an apartment. For unfurnished dwellings, the Braves reimburse players for the rental of a bed, chest of drawers, lamp, dinette and sofa, but not a television, VCR, stereo or cable television service. When a player is promoted during the season, he is lucky if the newcomer taking his roster spot will step in and pick up the expenses. Otherwise, the Braves and the player are left to haggle over who owes what to whom.

While day-to-day living offers challenges to players in their late teens, professional baseball presents even more hurdles that few players ever consider. Most players have played the game since the formidable days of childhood, but never have they taken the field for games on a daily basis, from early spring through the dog days of August. Macon's schedule, for example, began April 7 and continued through September 4, barring an appearance in the playoffs. During those five months, the Braves have nine days off, three of those coming during the South Atlantic League all-star break June 19-21.

"You got to have a tremendous want-to, a strive for excellence, an inner drive," Roberts said. "You got to be a warrior, you got to be mentally tough. There's a lot of success stories out there about guys with medium types of tools who turn themselves into decent ballplayers. You need to watch those guys, the overachievers."

Other hurdles play mind games with young players. Some feel the pressure of playing for a paycheck instead of playing for recreation. Many hitters experience difficulty swinging a wooden bat as opposed to the more powerful aluminum weapons used in the amateur ranks. Another challenge hitters have is facing a good pitcher every evening as opposed to one or two a season. Then there is the feeling that they are living in a fish bowl, with their performances graded every night, their value constantly evaluated.

In essence, minor-league baseball offers top-flight competition, even at the lowest levels. Every player has a lifetime worth of glory days. Many have never sustained any hardships on the diamond prior to turning pro and encountering the daily grind that is baseball in the minors.

No one needed to remind any of the Macon Braves about hardships. The team's losing ways continued in the opener at Macon's Luther Williams Field, with Savannah taking a 4-1 decision. Sunday afternoon brought more of the same, a 4-2 win for the Cardinals, although the Braves had the tying run at the plate and Dye at second base with one out in the bottom of the eighth inning. Macon failed to capitalize, however, when third baseman John Knott and first baseman Randall Simon both flied out to center field to end the threat.

"We stayed in the game," Roberts said, brandishing a grin that showed little concern. "We came close to hitting a couple balls out that would have made a difference. With any kind of luck at all, things are going to turn around."

The hoped-for good fortune did not take place on Monday, April 11. Albany overcame a splendid pitching performance from Mathews by manufacturing a run in the sixth to win the game, 3-2. Macon's losing streak extended to six games on Tuesday after the Braves wasted strong pitching outings from Esteban Yan and David Wells by failing to drive home runners in scoring position in four of the nine innings for a 1-0 Polecat victory.

A win didn't take place on Wednesday, either, a 5-3 defeat at Columbus, or the next day, a 6-1 loss to the RedStixx. King's eighth-inning home run, the first of his professional career and the initial roundtripper of the season for the Macon team, was not enough to break the streak at nine on Friday, with Capital City holding on to a 3-2 win at Luther Williams Field. By the time the Braves were filing on the bus and heading for their longest road trip of the season, a nine-day jaunt to Asheville, North Carolina, and Charleston, West Virginia, their record stood at 0-10, making them the only winless team in professional baseball.

The last few days tied Roberts' stomach into one large knot. His concerns centered not on how the team's performance might reflect on him, but the effect constant losing could have on the development of the players. Riding in the first seat of the bus, Roberts flipped through a couple books on motivation and positive approaches, books that he and coach Glenn Hubbard obtained at the Macon library in an effort to right a ship that started along the wrong path.

His concerns notwithstanding, Roberts did not lose his positive reinforcement. Not once did he rant and rave at his players. Baseball is a game in which the players must play relaxed. Too much tension and nervousness puts a lock on the flow and the immediate mental decisions needed to throw accurately to the right base, hang with a breaking ball or make the proper pitch on a 3-and-2 count with runners in scoring position.

There was another reason Roberts did not have to scare his players. Many members of the Braves' minor-league staff invaded Asheville shortly after the Macon bus arrived in the "Paris of the South." Their presence provided a warning the equivalent of an air horn blown six inches from a player's ear. Holed up in the Days Inn, the staff including Bobby Dews, assistant director of player development Rod Gilbreath, scouting and player development assistant Scott Proefrock, roving catching instructor Joe Szekely, and strength and conditioning coach Ken Crenshaw met with Roberts, Hubbard and Macon pitching coach Larry Jaster to determine what players were treading water and making progress, and who was on the verge of drowning. The extra staff also allowed for more one-on-one work with various players prior to the games. That enabled Roberts to get a few second opinions while dealing with those he felt needed special attention.

"We're just trying to see what we've got," Gilbreath said. "We knew when they came in here that they were going to struggle a little bit. They just got off to a slow start. But I guarantee you, the second half they're going to make great strides. They understand that. We just can't let them get down. So we're just in here watching them and making a few adjustments here and there."

Those adjustments failed to alter recent history during the first evening at McCormick Field. Macon spotted the Tourists a seven-run lead before falling short with a three-inning rally to lose, 7-6. The Braves made it 12 straight on Monday night, dropping a 3-0 decision to the hosts. As the team boarded the bus to return to the motel, a few heads started to hang for the first time.

Tuesday, April 19, began similar to the previous 12 days. The Tourists jumped out to a 2-0 lead in the first inning. Not to be outdone, the Braves fought back to trail 3-2 after six frames before justice finally prevailed. Lance Marks, a 23-year-old veteran who joined the team in Asheville on a rehabilitation assignment, drove in three runs. Jacobs hurled $4^1/_3$ innings of solid relief so that when Marcus Hostetler registered the final out and a save in the truest sense, many of the unknowing spectators might have thought a championship had been won. The Braves poured onto the field before showering one another with soft drinks in the visiting clubhouse, all because a 7-3 win had improved the team's record to 1-12.

"When you start the season as bad as we have, it just makes it that much more difficult," said John Knott, one of just three players to return to Macon from 1993. "Until tonight, things just haven't been going right. Our pitching, our hitting, nothing is there at the same time. The first four or five innings are the toughest. After that, it seems like we're saying, 'We can play with these guys.' From the sixth inning on, we're tough as nails. We're just having a tough time overcoming what happens during those first five innings."

A night later, it was back to the same ol' same ol'. In fact, it would be nine more days before Macon would register another notch in the win column. The Braves dropped the final game in Asheville prior to being swept by the Wheelers in a four-game series. During the Braves' visit to West Virginia, a few tense moments took place along the country roads. Some of the Charleston players heckled Macon during batting practice, some to the point of wondering aloud how the Braves were able to coax a contract out of Atlanta. Before boys could be boys, Roberts rallied his troops and kept everyone under control.

"Fellas, if we keep doing our job, doing what we've been doing, we'll have the final laugh," Roberts said. "They're trying to piss you guys off and cause us to lose our concentration. If they do, we don't have a chance."

While the Braves may have taken heed of Roberts' advice, once the Macon bus departed Watt Powell Park for the final time, the team stood 1-17, a full 15 games behind first-place Savannah. Labelled by *The Macon Telegraph* as "lovable losers," the Braves exuded little goodwill and harmony on the 521-mile bus trip back to Middle Georgia. The team, to a player, was thoroughly embarrassed.

Macon Madness

6

The sun had emerged from the horizon when the Macon bus pulled into the parking lot of Luther Williams Field. Leon Roberts repeatedly told his team during the season's first 2½ weeks that tomorrow was a new day. No one had trouble believing the skipper on Monday, April 25, for that was the first day off the Braves would enjoy since the season of dreams had built into one collective nightmare.

Roberts knew his players needed some time away from baseball, and responded by giving them the day off. And while most observers would have called him crazy, the skipper was encouraged in recent games. "Probably the best sign is that in the face of adversity, we haven't caved in," Roberts said. "Of the 18 games we've played, we had a chance in 14 of them. That shows we're getting there, that we're close. And the players are still doing their work, keeping their spirits up. It's been rough, but they've been doing a good job of hanging in and going out there."

A 1-17 start would be tantamount to suicide in attracting fans at the major-league level. In the minors, while a dismal won-lost record is not fatal, there are ramifications. The energy and excitement typically garnered from winning is nonexistent, thereby keeping the masses away from the yard. As for those that do venture out, a few might begin to ride the home team a little harder than normal.

"I don't think winning makes that much difference, except maybe to the die-hard fans," said Macon general manager Ed Holtz, who has had his fair share of poor teams to promote during his 32-year career in baseball operations. "We get lots of people out here with groups from work and their bosses are buying their meals and their drinks. They could care less how the team is doing night in and night out."

That indifference did not keep a few fans from voicing their opinions. Before the Braves returned home from their road trip, some letters had appeared in *The Macon Telegraph*, with the authors making assumptions that a local high school team could easily handle the club that inhabited Luther Williams Field. Although the authors were obviously unschooled as to the amount of talent even the worst minor-league teams possess, the comments did little for the players' attitude toward the city.

"The fans here don't have a clue as to what's going on," John Knott said. "You can't even call them fans. Hardly any of them come to the stadium, and those that do just come here to kick somebody when they're down. I know I shouldn't let it bother me, and I know they have a right to cheer or boo when they come here. But to just come here and jump all over guys who are busting their butts isn't right.

"They say they'd support a team if we were winning, but that's just an excuse. This city doesn't deserve a team. They don't know anything about us because they don't take the time to try."

The Macon fans were not the only ones exuding frustration. Knott had felt the fury since discovering he would be back in Macon in 1994. Like Tim Gillis in Greenville, Knott's role was to serve as a veteran leader for a young group of players. But while Gillis accepted the responsibility, Knott despised it. He wanted to be in Durham, playing alongside his friends, the same players he called teammates in Macon a year earlier.

"That's what I was looking so forward to in spring training. You always hear about the Bulls and The Dap. I thought it'd be neat to play there. Hopefully I'll get that chance this season. You never know. Anything can happen in this game. Somebody gets hurt, you never know," Knott said.

Knott's frustration had actually been building for more than a year. Signed out of a Houston tryout camp in February 1993 after being overlooked in the draft following his final season at Southwest Missouri State, the versatile infielder received an early surprise during his first year when he was assigned to Macon instead of one step lower, at Idaho Falls. But Knott's bliss led to a rapid education in the world of player development. He found himself sitting on the bench, playing behind Robert Smith, a young third baseman the Braves viewed as a prospect. And while Knott outperformed Smith in most phases of the game, the hands of then-Macon manager Randy Ingle were tied. Orders from above dictated that Smith play the hot corner, not Knott.

By midseason, Knott began to openly question the politics of the situation. A few of his teammates even came to his defense. Ingle had little leverage, yet he did what most other managers would not have bothered to do. Ingle sat down with Knott and told him in as straight-forward a manner as possible what they were up against.

"Randy told me there's two games in baseball. There's the one on the field and the one off the field, trying to figure out what the front office is doing with players, who they're moving, and why they're playing this guy and not that guy," Knott said. "Randy told me that when he was playing, he tried to figure it out. He said as soon as he thought he had it figured out, he realized he didn't have anything right. That's what I was doing, trying to figure out what was going on instead of concentrating on what was taking place on the field. You just have to let what happens off the field happen and do your best on the field."

John Knott was not a happy camper when he returned to Macon to open the 1994 season. (Photo courtesy of Macon Braves)

No one needed to tell Knott that he failed to follow that advice during the early stages of the 1994 campaign. His batting average was a mere .160 heading into the final week of April. On the positive side, he was no longer pulling splinters out of his rear. He was taking the field every night, and the Braves did not have another prospect on the horizon to send Knott back to the pines.

Given the Braves' record, it was not a surprise that nearly every Macon player was struggling with the bat, including Knott's defensive partner on the left side of the infield, Danny Magee. A shortstop with a lanky but maturing build with a cannon attached to the right shoulder, Magee had been inconsistent with the glove and at the plate. His batting average stood at an unimpressive .194, and he paced the Braves in errors, a feat that had been hard to achieve considering the team's sloppy performances in the field. Yet, for a 19-year-old kid who was playing on the high school diamonds in and around Denham Springs, Louisiana, less than a year ago, Magee had already garnered a mature grasp of what was taking place.

"I'm the type of player who wants to do too much," Magee said. "I want to go every day full-force. Now I'm beginning to realize that everything isn't going to go your way every day. I've hit the ball good at times this year, but they're not finding holes. So I try to get my hits when I can.

"I never realized that last year, because I only played about 20 games, and my back was hurting the whole season. All through high school you dominated; you're used to doing well. When you get here, there's pitchers that shut you down. You might go through streaks 0-for-12, 0-for-15. I've already done that once this season, and I absolutely lost it because I've never been through it. Now that I've gone through it, I became a better player."

Scouts expected Magee to waste little time before showing major-league ability in the minors. There were some questions, however, surrounding the clean-cut blond whose peach fuzz makes him look even younger than he is. One centered on his willingness to sign a professional contract out of high school. A full ride at the University of New Orleans awaited, and Magee gave the offer full consideration. Then there was the issue regarding which position he would play as a professional. Primarily a shortstop, he also pitched for his high school team. Magee could bring it to the plate in the low 90s, figures that will catch a scout's attention faster than a low-cut blouse and a high-riding skirt.

Danny Magee discovered how difficult playing baseball every day can be for a young prospect. (Photo courtesty of Macon Braves)

In the days leading up to the 1993 draft, scouts from the Dodgers and Marlins expressed the greatest interest, with both teams thinking of putting Magee on the mound. But when the telephone rang at his home on June 1, Braves scout Deric Ladnier was calling to inform Magee that he had been plucked by Atlanta in the sixth round.

While he anticipated the chain of events, Magee soon found himself faced with the most difficult decision of his life to that point. He had always envisioned attending college, and UNO was offering to foot the entire bill. At the same time, his dream was similar to those of other young boys who take countless ground balls in the sweltering summer sun instead of improving their tans alongside bikini-clad admirers at the local pool. He wanted a shot at playing pro ball, and Ladnier was pushing a Braves contract across the table with an opportunity to do just that.

Magee did not rush his decision. He took a week or so to weigh the choices, to grasp what it was he really wanted to do. When the Braves sweetened the deal by offering a college tuition package on top of a significant signing bonus, the scales began to tip, and Magee was packing for West Palm Beach.

"When I first signed, I kept saying, 'Did I make the right choice?'" said Magee, who played in the Gulf Coast and Appalachian leagues in 1993. "After I had been out there for a couple of weeks, I knew that's what I wanted to do.

It's baseball every day. And if you love baseball, go for it. You still got to work at it, because the one difference is everybody can play here. If you were the type of player in high school that loved being the standout, when you get here, you better get used to it quick that everybody can play and that you're just part of a great team.

"You really don't do much other than play baseball. You wake up, you get out on the field around 3:30, you take BP, then you play a game. It's a great lifestyle. It took me a month or so to get into it because I was used to playing two or three days a week. But once you get used to it, nothing can beat this life.

"This is player development. You're going to do things wrong in order to improve. You got to understand you learn from your mistakes. They don't expect you to come in here and tear it up. If you just come in here and play your best, everything will take care of itself. That's what everyone on this team has to realize."

Magee's realizations were not the only thing that had come together in rapid fashion. The shortstop's positive outlook spread to his teammates, making him one of the team's most popular players. The coaching staff had also taken notice, especially Glenn Hubbard, whose 12 years as a major-league second baseman helped him appreciate significant talent among shortstops.

"I played with Andres Thomas in Atlanta," Hubbard said. "He had the best tools. But when he got to the big leagues, he shut his work habits down. That's the biggest adjustment for some of these kids, especially the high school kids. Growing up, they went out on the diamond and dominated by just being there. God gave them great ability. When you get here, everyone dominated. So now you got to work and apply and make adjustments. Making adjustments, that might be the biggest thing.

"Danny, great work habits, love for the game, intensity. It's hard to find. You can turn down a flame, but it's hard to start a flame with a guy. It's like striking a wet match. Danny has that fire. Sometimes I got to bring it down for fear he's going to blow up. He's gotten better at it, because he has great work habits. He's got a great arm. He listens and applies whatever you say. Give me those traits and his skills and I'll show you a kid that's going to make it."

Making it to the majors at this point in their careers is merely in the back of Magee's and his teammates' minds. Their concerns as April came to a close were salvaging any remaining respect they had as professional players while continuing to develop through the organization.

Most of that development was taking place at Luther Williams Field, located in the rear of Macon's City Park. Built in 1929, making it the second-oldest ballpark in the minors, and named after a former mayor, Luther Williams Field was welcomed into the sport when then-baseball commissioner Kenesaw Mountain Landis threw out the ceremonial first pitch. Since then, Macon served as a member of either the Sally and Southern leagues through the 1967 campaign, with its primary claim to fame coming as Pete Rose's final minor-league stop in 1962 before his ascent to Cincinnati. After enduring the national epidemic that saw minor-league baseball survive in just a handful of cities and teeter on the brink of extinction in the 1970s, the pro game returned to Macon in 1980 before leaving again in 1987.

When the Pirates' affiliate opted for greener financial pastures in Augusta, Georgia, in 1987, many figured that the final fans had entered the brick-and-iron front gates of Luther Williams Field. The common brick structure had cracks in the same manner an old face shows wrinkles. Its facilities were small, outdated and worn out, providing little more than memories of what had been instead of hope for what could be.

One person who failed to lose that hope for future memories was Harley Bowers, the longtime sports editor of *The Macon Telegraph*. Bowers has a love for baseball that dates beyond his days in the 1950s as public relations director for the St. Louis Cardinals' minor-league training camp in Albany, Georgia, an outfit headed by Branch Rickey, the founding father of the minors. Bowers looked at Luther Williams Field as a showcase for the sport, a museum that still had some history to make. Refusing to let the ballpark become a haven for undesirables before eventually meeting the crushing blows of a wrecking ball, Bowers began a campaign to bring minor-league baseball back to Macon.

Bowers' efforts took four years before his dream became reality. He contacted every major-league organization before striking paydirt 90 miles north on Interstate 75. The Southern gentleman convinced the Braves to move their Class A team from Sumter, South Carolina, where fan support had been virtually nonexistent, to Macon. Atlanta even put $800,000 into renovating Luther Williams Field. The result is one of baseball's quaintest ballparks, a 3,500-seat theater, complete with a bronze plaque honoring Bowers for his troubles.

Equally advantageous is the relationship Atlanta and Macon share. Atlanta benefits by having a team in close proximity to the parent club. Macon, meanwhile, is helped by the great success the Braves have enjoyed in recent years, even if the major-league team is often the primary competition for the minor-league Braves. Practically everyone in the area is a Braves fan, and Luther Williams Field offers Atlanta's stars of tomorrow today.

"I think the closeness to Atlanta not only helps our fan support, but it also creates more responsibility on both sides since the boss is nearby," Holtz said. "They see the things we need, and we are better able to do things in a way the Braves want them done."

Those reasons are why owning farm teams has become an attractive alternative for major-league franchises compared to the relationships with sometimes-fickle minor-league club owners. Various necessities are paid for out of one primary operating budget, reducing headaches on both sides.

"It's a tremendous advantage for a guy in my position," Holtz said. "For 20 years I was on the other side. I had to go to the owner and tell him I needed $2,600 for meal money by Friday night, and his response would be, 'You better go out and sell some advertising.' That's bullshit.

"Here, I know the bills are going to be paid. We're not rich, but the Braves know that certain things are needed to operate a club. It's a great relationship."

Most of the Macon fans do not realize that their team is owned by Ted Turner's vast empire. Part of that stems from the fact that Holtz and his wife, Mary, operate the team and its front-office staff of five in a mom 'n pop manner not unlike the days when Luther Williams Field was in its prime. Ed, a graying, stocky man often donned in suspenders, has served as general manager of Wausau, Chattanooga, Knoxville and Sumter, and handles the day-to-day operations. Mary answers the telephone, points Ed in the right direction and runs the office from the top of the grandstand during games.

"Macon's a good town, but you have to prove yourself," Holtz said. "I guess the hardest thing I've had to adjust to is the fact that Southerners are so damn polite. It takes three, four phone calls because people are afraid to tell you no. I'm a Midwesterner who wants to tell it like it is. If you aren't going to buy a fence sign, just tell me. But if your car breaks down, this is the place to have it happen. People here are always so willing to help. There's so much charity here, it's incredible. Most places I've lived, people are afraid to help others for fear of getting mugged or something. Not here."

Holtz's style, a little too straightforward for some of the locals, is similar to the way he markets his baseball team. In these days of outrageous and expensive promotions featured in many minor-league parks, Holtz prefers that baseball be the main attraction. Some of that stems from his experience and beliefs, some comes from the budget he is provided by the Braves. So instead of forking out $6,000 to bring in The Famous Chicken or another high-priced act, Holtz opts for giving the first 200 moms a flower on Mother's Day, helping the WR Optimists with their fund-raiser and handing out two-for-one beverages every Thursday. Those promotions lead to more than 100,000 fans clicking the turnstiles annually since the Braves came to town.

Holtz's work does little to overcome the fact that no one wants to be associated with a loser, even in the minors. While Roberts was faced with more challenges than any man should have to confront, Holtz met nearly as many hurdles in attracting fans. The team had not helped matters by dropping a 5-3 decision to Hagerstown in its first game back home before exploding for its largest run output of the season, nine runs, four coming on a grand slam by Knott, only to lose by one.

Finally, on April 28, nearly three weeks after the season opened, the Braves gave the home fans something to cheer. Wonderful Terrific Monds III, an outfielder selected in the 50th and final round of the 1993 draft, broke the team's seven-game home losing streak by driving a ball down the right-field line. Hagerstown outfielder Lorenzo De La Cruz failed in his attempted shoestring catch, and watched the ball roll to the field's deepest corner. Monds raced around the bases, nearly catching Jermaine Dye in the process, for a three-run, inside-the-park home run in the Braves' 6-1 triumph.

Friday night saw Macon win back-to-back games for the first time, taking a 6-0 decision over the Suns. Knott and newcomer Feliberto Selmo, promoted a day earlier when Randall Simon was placed on the disabled list, combined to drive home five of the six runs, while Carey Paige continued to emerge as a prospect, allowing just two hits and no walks while fanning six in a half-dozen innings of work.

Unlike the postgame ceremony following the win in Asheville, the Macon players did not spray one another with soft drinks after earning their first split of the season. Instead, even with a 3-19 record, confidence was slowly becoming evident. April was one day away from becoming May.

"I think everyone was getting sick and tired of losing," said Paige, his sweat-filled hair nearly covering a pair of eyes in the initial stages of forming a hungry, confident look. "We just had to hang in there, and now we're starting to get into a groove. We know we can win now. We've known all along that we're a good team. Now everything is coming together."

Wade-ing Pool

7

Steve DeSalvo paced throughout Greenville Municipal Stadium like an expectant father. For three weeks the G-Braves' general manager had been contemplating, preparing for and fretting about the series April 25-27 that would produce the largest three-day attendance in the Double-A team's 11-year history.

"It's going to be a regular three-ring circus around here," DeSalvo told his employees on the Sunday prior to the series. "I've even thought about bringing in some elephants, but I guess we really don't need anything to add to what's about to happen."

The event was three games between Greenville and the visiting Birmingham Barons. That was what DeSalvo focused on, baseball games. At no time during the three weeks, when nearly 24,000 tickets were sold, did he mention any of the game's possible participants, especially Baron outfielder Michael Jordan, the reason for DeSalvo's nervous behavior and the South Carolina city's frenzied anticipation.

Recent history had much to do with DeSalvo's state. No matter which Southern League city the Michael Jordan Tour had taken the Barons to in the opening weeks of the season, the response had been chaotic. In Birmingham's first road game, the Chattanooga Lookouts allowed 13,416 fans to enter the gates of 7,500-seat Historic Engel Stadium. Jordan didn't play, and riots nearly erupted. The Nashville Xpress drew 16,842 fans for a two-game series, while the Carolina Mudcats welcomed a standing room-only gathering of 8,045, more than 2,000 above Five County Stadium's capacity.

In the press box an hour before the G-Braves would conclude a three-game stint with the Lookouts on April 24, Matt Garvey was on the verge of collapsing. Even his upbeat assistant, Sean O'Connor, showed hints of being on the wrong end of a colossal beating. The two had been deluged with more than 100 press credential requests from throughout the eastern half of the United States. For a team that considers a large turnout to be five writers covering a game in a press box that can barely accommodate 10 people comfortably, the 81 credential recipients would have to be situated in the top rows of the stands behind home plate, leaving Garvey with having to play one incredibly large game of musical chairs.

The requests were just part of what was increasing Garvey's stress level with every phone call. Jordan, considered by most observers to be one of the greatest basketball players of our time before oddly deciding to retire from the National Basketball Association and take up baseball at age 31, was making himself available for interviews on an extremely limited basis. No one, including Garvey and the Birmingham roadies, was sure what Jordan's self-established rules would be in Greenville. Garvey hoped the outfielder would hold a press conference either before or after the first game, but he had no way of gaining an answer, which did little to satisfy the salivating media.

On the field, the Greenville players, off to a solid 9-5 start on the season, were low-key about the imminent situation. A few were excited, but no one seemed to be on the brink of duplicating what a couple Lookouts did in Chattanooga. With Jordan out of the lineup, two players went over to the Birmingham dugout between innings and asked for the star's autograph. Instead, Jordan's presence meant playing in front of three straight full houses, events that get the blood flowing through any athlete's body.

Jordan's primary sport is the same one Terrell Wade concentrated on during his high school days in Rembert, South Carolina, population 350. Wade gave baseball little of his time, playing only during his senior year and immediately afterwards in American Legion ball. Though big for a left-hander at 6-foot-3 and at least 200 pounds, Wade did not impress the few scouts that saw him pitch. His fastball registered only 80 miles an hour, good for the prep ranks but barely mediocre for the pros. In fact, just one scout, Montreal's Fred Wright, spent any significant time with Wade. Wright showed the young pitcher two grips, one for a better fastball, another for a slider, a pitch Wade had never attempted.

The tips made Wade a better pitcher during American Legion games in the early summer days of 1991. His efforts became so strong that a teammate and coach convinced Wade to travel to nearby Sumter on June 17 and attend a tryout camp that Braves scout Roy Clark was holding. After some prodding, Wade made the trip.

Clark was immediately impressed with Wade, so much so that he asked the pitcher to travel to Charleston, South Carolina, and throw again the following day. Wade refused, telling Clark that he had to pitch for his team on Sunday. The scout asked Wade where he lived and for his telephone number. He also asked the youngster if he would be interested in playing professional baseball. "I said, 'I don't see nothing wrong with it,'" Wade recalled.

Within minutes after the tryout camp, Clark was on the telephone with Chuck LaMar. Clark was adamant about signing the southpaw. LaMar trusted Clark's judgment and agreed. The hard part came when Clark began searching for Wade in Rembert. A few phone calls and directions from locals landed the scout in a pool hall, where Wade was continuing a family tradition as one of the town's best sharks.

Signed to a professional contract on a pool table, Terrell Wade quickly became a scout's dream. (Photo courtesy of Greenville Braves)

Clark approached Wade and said he wanted to sign the pitcher right there, complete with a $5,000 bonus. Most 18-year-olds would have stopped anything to sign such a contract; Wade said it would have to wait. In the meantime, he ran the table, collected his winnings from his opponent, then walked over to Clark and earned five grand by signing his deal on a pool table not in use.

Shortly after coming to terms with the Braves in 1991, Wade was off to West Palm Beach, where his raw talents showed potential but a need for significant refinement. His earned run average was a high 6.26, although his 22 strikeouts in 23 innings were promising. The 1992 season proved to be a carbon copy at Idaho Falls, with the lefty winning just one of five decisions, and fanning 54 in 50$^{1}/_{3}$ frames. Again there were glimmers of hope, yet nothing that would keep a pitcher employed much longer.

"Those two years, I had no mechanics and I wasn't staying focused," Wade said. "I hadn't proved to Atlanta that I could pitch as well as I can. Then at the end of spring training in 1993, I told the guys that I was going to have a good season. They said, 'How do you know?' I said, 'I'm getting my fastball down, I'm getting everything else over. The way I look at it, I can't be touched.'"

South Atlantic League hitters soon seconded Wade's notion. He overpowered the circuit's lumbermen during the first three months of the season by posting an 8-2 record and a 1.73 ERA in 14 starts. Along the way he fanned 18 hitters in one game, a minor-league best for the 1993 campaign. A promotion to Durham followed in addition to a 2-1 mark and Carolina League pitcher-of-the-week honors for July 4-10. He then wrapped up the organization's Phil Niekro Award, representing Atlanta's minor-league pitcher of the year, by tossing eight games and going 2-1 with a 3.21 ERA at Greenville. For the year he was 12-4 with 208 strikeouts, a total that ranked second in the minors.

Those accomplishments propelled Wade to the top of baseball's prospects list. Naturally, there were critics who thought the lefty was simply a one-year wonder. Many of those came out of the woodwork when Wade stumbled during big league camp. Overweight and out of synch, he struggled with his control and was quickly returned to the minor-league side of the West Palm Beach complex.

"I came in a little heavy, but I didn't let that affect me," Wade said after the season started. "I worked on my weight hard, and I learned my lesson. But negative stuff, all I do is block it out. I don't let it get to me because most of the time people are going to write what they want to in the paper anyway. That don't bother me. I'm just going to stay Terrell Wade and go out and do what I got to do."

It was obvious that Wade's rise to stardom had not changed his personality. He was without question the most playful, easygoing and popular player on the Greenville roster. If he was not impersonating someone, he was wrestling with a teammate, threatening to body slam him to the ground. That rambunctiousness makes him the target of much kidding. "Hey, Terrell, I called that gay bar like you asked me to," outfielder Kevin O'Connor interrupted during one of Wade's many interviews. "They are closed on Monday, but they said they'd be ready for you on Tuesday." Wade responded with a snicker, then began thinking of how he would gain revenge, practically forgetting about the interview in process.

That kind of playfulness attracted additional criticism. Several opposing Southern League managers and coaches wondered aloud if Wade had the desire to improve his game to the point where he could consistently compete in the majors. So far, those comments had little bearing on the results. Wade pitched well during his first two appearances of the season before becoming a sacrificial lamb in his third start. An extra-inning game in Huntsville that was eventually suspended after 12 frames prevented the Greenville bus from reaching Memphis prior to six the following morning. A one o'clock start meant Wade took the mound against the Chicks with less than three hours' sleep, and the results showed. In three innings, he surrendered nine earned runs on seven hits and five walks.

"I had a rough outing, but I don't blame it on nobody," Wade said. "I don't blame it on the bus ride. I just didn't have my good stuff that day. In the back of my mind, I just made a note and said the next time I face them, I owe them a little something."

Under more normal circumstances, Wade continued to prove that he was still an overpowering prospect. On the eve of Jordan's arrival, the southpaw dominated the Lookouts, tossing six strong innings and allowing just two hits and one run while fanning eight. He also helped his cause in the 5-1 Greenville victory when he took Calvain Culberson's fastball the opposite way and deposited it over the left-field fence. That feat turned out to be one that Wade's teammates heard about for the remainder of the season.

A night later, the hoopla surrounding Jordan and the Barons created a few cases of the jitters on the part of the G-Braves. Jason Schmidt, who entered the game with a 2-0 record and an 0.82 ERA, was touched for three runs by the Barons in the second inning. Birmingham added another three-spot in the fifth, with Jordan extending his hitting streak to 12 games with a clean single, driving home two base runners. Jordan also displayed his defensive skills in right field with an impressive diving catch in the second inning.

But the Barons' six-run advantage did not hold up. Tony Graffanino produced a three-run double and Ed Giovanola's two-tally single ignited a seven-run seventh for the G-Braves, guiding the home team to its 10th triumph in 13 outings. The crowd situation proved relatively uneventful, and Garvey's worries were calmed somewhat when Jordan emerged from the left-field clubhouse a half-hour after the game and monotonically talked to reporters for 10 minutes.

"I think I'm improving every game, which is the way I want it to be," said Jordan, whose batting average was a startling .326. "It's going to take some more time, which is one of the reasons I'm still here. I have a lot to learn about the game. Each and every day I feel I'm learning more and more. I think I've surprised a lot of people, but I believed in myself from the start. That's something to build on."

Unfortunately for Jordan, that spring evening proved to be close to the pinnacle of the season for the most popular Baron. After upping his hitting streak to 13 games a night later, when the G-Braves came from behind again and won their seventh straight contest, 4-3, Jordan fell into a horrendous slump, caused largely by the effectiveness of Southern League pitchers' curveballs. The former guard took the collar on the third and final game of the series, a 3-1 win for Birmingham, then watched his batting average tumble all the way into the high one hundreds before concluding the campaign with a hitting norm of .202.

His hitting prowess less than advantageous for the Baron attack, Jordan did prove to be a godsend for the team and the league. Contrary to most reports, he did not buy a luxury bus for Birmingham, but did use his pull to help acquire a spiffy model that had plenty of leg room, even for Jordan's 6-foot-6 frame. His presence also enabled Birmingham to establish a league record by attracting 467,868 fans to Hoover Metropolitan Stadium in 1994. In addition, nearly 2.6 million fans flocked to Southern League ballparks during the campaign, a mark that set the circuit's single-season attendance record.

On the diamond, the response was equally positive and unanimous, at least for Jordan's effort if not the results. "I was glad to see his work ethic," said Bruce Benedict. "But you know what I really like? I sense in him that playing baseball is really fun for him. I think he's done with his job. I think he's just playing this game and working hard at it and really enjoying it."

The same thing could be said about Benedict's G-Braves, who owned a three-game lead over Jacksonville in the league's Eastern Division. Even if the hitters had scored the second-fewest runs in the league and were having a hard time living up to the team's marketing slogan, "Bats On Fire," the defense was nearly airtight, and the pitching was the circuit's best.

Success continued in the next series with Memphis. Following a defeat after an off day, Wade lived up to his promise of gaining revenge versus the Chicks. The left-hander tossed seven shutout innings of four-hit ball, striking out nine opponents in Greenville's 2-1 triumph. That win gave the G-Braves a 13-6 record for April, fueling hopes for bigger things in the season's final four months.

8 A Bat Out of Hell

Bud Waldrop could not remember feeling as exhausted yet as exhilarated as he was on this mild, late April evening. Not exactly fresh after a 13-hour, 885-mile drive that began in the bleary hours in Decatur, Illinois, wound across half of Tennessee, up and over the Smoky Mountains, and across most of North Carolina before concluding at Durham Athletic Park, the white flat-topped man with warm blue eyes refused to collapse midway in the front row of the 20 blue seats reserved for scouts, certain journalists and chosen fans behind home plate. Bud Waldrop did not make the journey to rest at trip's end; he came to watch and talk some baseball.

"My son's number thirty-three, Tom Waldrop," the player's father said in a coarse, friendly voice. He paused for a moment and watched the tall left-hander take a few cuts in the batting cage. "I get goose bumps when Tommy hits a home run or throws a guy out from the outfield. There's nothing I'd rather see. Nothing. That's the ultimate thrill for me."

Tom Waldrop had been providing his dad as well as all Durham fans with plenty of chills. Following a rough spring and a rougher start to the season that spawned a dismal .074 batting average, the right fielder clubbed the team's first grand slam of the campaign in the Bulls' 11-4 win at Salem five days earlier. Two nights later, in Winston-Salem, he equalled the feat by swatting his second jack with the bases drunk. By the time his father pulled into town just prior to Friday's sunset, Waldrop had registered 10 hits and 13 runs batted in during his last 23 at bats.

Waldrop's one-man wrecking crew did not come a game too early for the Bulls. Neither the team's pitching nor the hitting was consistent during the first 2½ weeks of the season, an inept combination that dropped the Bulls to the cellar in the Carolina League's Southern Division with a 5-10 record. Kevin Grijak, owner of a league-best .404 batting average and eight home runs, was the lone steady producer with the lumber, only to have a knee injury land him on the sidelines for the past week. But thanks to Waldrop's upstart efforts, Durham was playing its best baseball of the season when it entered the weekend series with first-place Wilmington.

"I was feeling around in the beginning, trying to find what worked for me," said the younger Waldrop. "When we came back after the first road trip, I was able to come out here early every day and I kind of found my balance in my swing. I started feeling a little bit more confident about myself and things came together. Before, I was going up there being overaggressive and anxious, not getting a good pitch to hit. Now I'm going up there and taking it one at bat at a time, not trying to get nine hits in two at bats. If I don't get hits my first two at bats, I'm not going to waste the other two by pressing. If I just play my game, I should have success."

Any success Waldrop had on the field as well as in life can be traced to his parents, Bud and Sally. Adopted when he was just four days old, Tom grew up as an only child in a middle-class family in the heart of the Midwest. His father brought home the bacon and paid the mortgage as an insurance salesman before tiring of the business and moving to used car lots. Those jobs helped finance Tom's baseball career, one that Bud estimates comes close to $100,000 after equipment, camps and everything else is added up.

Waldrop's dreams of playing professional baseball took root on the Little League fields of Decatur. He showed promise at an early age, always providing his teams with a lethal one-two punch of power and pitching. Those abilities continued through his high school days and into college, initially at Iowa Western Community College and his final two years at Olivet Nazarene University. Through it all, his dreams were the same as they had been when he could first hoist a bat and swing it.

According to at least three scouts that visited Waldrop during the latter days of his junior season, his dreams were about to become reality during the annual amateur draft. One scout predicted Tom would be plucked in the first three rounds, and went so far as to tell Bud, "Your son is about to make you rich."

It didn't happen. Waldrop was not drafted because, according to that same scout, the player's index card had been inadvertently pulled when the team went to take him. That experience left Waldrop hopeful but leery after his senior year. He was confident that at least by the second day of the three-day affair that some team would be willing to give him a shot. With all the expectations of a child awaiting the arrival of Santa, Waldrop propped himself on the sofa and waited for the telephone to ring.

The telephone did ring on several occasions, proving that it was working. The problem was, none of the callers was associated with professional baseball. When the clock struck midnight on June 5, the final day of the draft, Waldrop had a pretty good idea how Cinderella was supposed to have felt.

"What am I going to do?" Tom asked his dad, though not searching for a concrete answer. "All I want to do is play baseball."

No player in the minor leageus was hotter than Tom Waldrop during the first week of May. (Photo courtesy of Durham Bulls)

"I tried to tell him that we'd do everything possible to make that dream come true," Bud recounted nearly two years later. "We'd send him to every camp, make every call that we could to make sure he got a chance just like we had always done. I also told him maybe it just wasn't meant to be, and maybe he ought to look into coaching at the high school level. Someone like the Braves might need a part-time scout. We'd do what we could to see that his dream came true."

Throughout high school, Waldrop had always been encouraged by his parents to find a part-time job. It somehow never materialized, mainly because Tom always focused his efforts on playing baseball, an alternative his parents accepted. That was a different time, however, and Tom was now faced with having to get a job for real. A few days later, Tom called his father at work.

"He said, 'Dad, I got a job,'" Bud recalled. "I was a little shocked, to be honest. I said, 'Yeah, what is it?' He said, 'It's with the Braves. I'm going to get a chance after all.'"

Atlanta scout Stu Cann reviewed the players he had scouted and found that the Olivet Nazarene product was still available. The Braves needed a couple players with college experience to complete the Idaho Falls roster, so Cann offered Waldrop a chance that included $1,000 to sign, up to $10,000 in bonuses if he reached the Double A and Triple A levels later in his career, and a plane ticket to the career of his dreams.

Waldrop had little trouble adapting to wooden bats and quickly proved his worth on the professional fields. He terrorized Pioneer League pitching by leading Idaho Falls with nine home runs and 45 runs batted in, and placed second on the team with a .311 batting average. A year later he made the jump to Macon and continued to have success with 11 roundtrippers and 52

RBIs, both of which were among the team's best before a late-season promotion to Durham.

"The Braves told me when they signed me that they needed power at the outfield corners and people to drive in runs from the left-hand side of the plate," Waldrop said. "When I was in Macon last year, I hit .246. Anybody would like for that to be a little bit higher, but my power numbers were good. I think I stayed pretty consistent through my first full season, which is the main key, going from rookie ball to long-season A."

Provided he had a good spring, Waldrop thought a promotion to Greenville would not be out of the question in 1994. Those hopes quickly vanished when the outfielder had trouble simply making contact in West Palm Beach. When camp broke and the Bulls headed north to Durham, Waldrop was mired in a slump so deep that he was just happy to be on the field, even if it meant splitting time with Grijak and Juan Williams. Finally, after Grijak succumbed to a bum knee, Waldrop took advantage of the opportunity and emerged as one of the primary power sources in the Bulls' lineup.

"I think the thrill about the grand slams was that I was able to do it when no one expected it," Waldrop said. "I know that my weakness in the scouting reports in this league has been to throw me away. Both of my grand slams were to left-center field on pitches that were on the outside corner. That's why I'm looking forward to playing those teams the second time. Salem and Winston-Salem, I'm hoping they will come in on me. That's always been my strength."

A week earlier, Waldrop's confidence was lower than a caterpillar's fuzz. Now, with the roller coaster ride taking him to the top, he could not wait to start swinging the bat. The baseball appeared to be the size of a pumpkin, and Waldrop was simply waiting for its approach and putting the ball where he wanted it.

Of course, the baseball is always the same size, and most pitches travel to the plate in similar paths. And while a batter's mechanics may determine to some extent how he performs, most of the success comes via the journeys that travel through the center of a player's mind. Baseball is at least 90 percent mental, a fact that Waldrop understood, even in the best of times.

"You can't be anxious in this game," Waldrop said. "You got to be laid back and realize that if you put up numbers, you'll move. Everybody here wants to do well and move up. But that can be your enemy, too. You start to press, all the sudden you're 0-for-15 and you're worried about your next 15."

That refurbished approach made Waldrop's first evening of the season playing in front of his father a little easier. He hit the ball hard, but took the collar in three trips to the plate against Wilmington's Mike Bovee, who cooled the league's hottest hitter as well as the rest of the Durham lineup by fanning 10 Bulls.

The 6-4 loss was more difficult for Matt Murray to accept. The right-hander came off his first win of the year the previous Sunday and hoped he was finally back on the right track. That was far from the case on Friday evening. Murray, who entered the game with a 4.64 ERA, surrendered six earned runs in $4^1/_3$ innings to post his third defeat. Among the tallies registered against him were a couple Ruthian blasts that cleared the center-field wall. Making matters worse were several borderline pitches that were all called balls by home plate umpire Ron Kulpa, along with at least three controversial plays called on the base paths by fellow blue Scott Higgins that went in favor of the Blue Rocks.

Yet none of those events could overshadow the fact that Murray was struggling. His pitches were being hit so hard that the grounds crew was on the verge of having to drag the warning track. He knew it, and he expressed his feelings upon being taken out of the game. Murray hurled his glove in the dugout, threw his cap to the ground, and grinded it into the dirt-covered concrete before sitting on the bench and dropping his face in his hands.

Deep down, Murray felt his career, including the desire to play, slipping away. The early promise in his career, the surgery, the rehab, everything seemed to be a distant memory. Maybe all those events, and now his struggles, were a signal. Maybe, Murray thought, it was time to quit fooling himself.

"After nights like last night, you really wonder if all the shit we go through is worth it," Murray said while charting pitches. "I haven't pitched well all year, and it's not like I'm doubting myself or anything. But it does make you think."

Most of Murray's thoughts center on his expectations. The pitcher, unhappy with his assignment to Durham, believed he would come to the Carolina League and prove the Braves had made a mistake, that he should have been assigned to Greenville to start the season. He fully expected to blow away the younger Class A hitters and dominate. That obviously had not happened.

The more he contemplated the situation, the more depressed he became. He talked continuously with his girl friend and soon-to-be fiancée, Nikki. Murray and Nikki met during spring training. A couple of chance meetings, first at the ballpark and later at a West Palm Beach shopping mall, ignited the romance. The pitcher had revealed his dreams to his new partner, a mild baseball fan at best. He told her of the paths he had traveled and where he had hoped the next one would take him. Despite her encouragement, he now felt he was on the road to nowhere.

Make no mistake, Nikki's listening and encouragement via long-distance phone calls and a couple of visits to Durham played a significant role in Murray's ability to cope with the situation. The same was true regarding another person involved in Murray's trials and tribulations, someone who had not stepped on the diamond since his childhood. Yet, his words after the pitcher's turbulent outing against Wilmington stuck with the right-hander.

"Last night, when I came out of the clubhouse, my priest from back home was waiting for me," Murray said. "He said, 'I was so proud of you. I know you didn't pitch as well as you would have liked, but I had tears in my eyes I was so proud. Just remember, you're living every little boy's dream.'

"He's really helped me, not only last night, but through the past couple years. When I came out today, I knew why I'm still pitching. Things are going to get better. Things aren't going good at all right now, but they will improve. If they don't, I'm not going to get out of Class A. But things will turn around."

As Murray continued to chart every pitch thrown, a chore all pitchers endure the night following a start, the tallies indicated that Durham hurler Blase Sparma was pitching the game he would later declare the best of his professional career. The right-hander tossed seven innings, allowed just two earned runs and seven hits before tiring and giving way to John Simmons, who held the Blue Rocks at bay in the Bulls' 10-3 win.

Sparma picked up his second win in twice as many decisions not only because of his performance on the mound, but also due to Waldrop's bat. After a one-night lull, the outfielder made every mile of his father's drive worthwhile. He doubled and scored Durham's first run on Ramon Nunez's single in the second inning, then cleared the right-field wall and struck the snorting bull, becoming just the third Durham hitter to dent the "Hit Bull, Win Steak" sign from a local steak restaurant. Waldrop's home run, his third of the week, brought a standing ovation and a little dance from his father, who exchanged winks with his son shortly after he crossed home plate.

Sunday afternoon, Bud patted his son on the back and headed to his seat prior to the game and his long trip back to Illinois. Last night's performance gave him something to talk about in Decatur until he would return to Durham later in the season, probably around the Fourth of July weekend. Of course, the topic was also up for discussion before he departed North Carolina.

"We went out and had a big celebration dinner last night," said Bud, his pride nearly bursting the buttons on his shirt. "I can see a big difference in Tommy this year. I could see it last year, too. Take a look at his first baseball card, the one at Idaho Falls. He's holding the bat low, kinda looking scared. Last year, he looks like a pro. The bat's held high, and he has that look of confidence in his eyes. That's the way he looks right now, ready to go."

Bud's words preceded the first start of the year by Darrell May, who emerged as one of the Braves' better pitching prospects in 1993 before opening the current campaign on the disabled list. May pitched admirably, surrendering just one run prior to exiting the game after reaching his pitch limit in the fifth inning. Then, as the case had been for much of the season's first month, the Bulls' relief corps gave the game away. Before the first out had been registered in the sixth, the Blue Rocks had crossed home plate 11 times. The most trying effort among the relievers was the one Ken Giard experienced. The right-hander faced six batters, retiring none. All eventually scored.

Wilmington's outburst brought the game to a virtual standstill. It was nearly four o'clock, and the senior Waldrop had 16 hours, 13 that would be spent behind the wheel, before he had to be at work. Though he remained in spirit, he gathered his belongings, walked behind the chain-link fence alongside The Dap and waved goodbye to his son standing in right field. He slid into the front seat of his Ford Taurus, worked his way through the streets of Durham, and began heading west along Interstate 40.

About a quarter-hour following his departure, Bud nearly drove his car off the highway while listening to the end of the Bulls' game on the radio. Tom had done it again, this time a three-run blast that landed on the roof of Brame Office Supplies, over the right-center field wall. A few innings later, Durham broadcaster Steve Barnes announced that Waldrop had been named co-Carolina League hitter of the week. "Something's wrong," added Barnes. "I can't for the life of me believe that someone has had a better week than Tom Waldrop."

Four home runs and 19 runs batted in during an eight-day span are the type of numbers usually produced only by children in backyard fantasy games. Tom Waldrop, meanwhile, was living a dream while chasing another. His only wish was that no one would awaken him.

Mordy's Cup of Coffee

9

Mike Mordecai sensed that his swing needed work. Though his bat had been one of the primary reasons for Richmond's 14-9 start, the shortstop had no desire to see his previous night's efforts — hitless in five trips to the plate during the R-Braves' 9-5 victory at Syracuse — become habit-forming. He had therefore decided to get up early, take the first bus to MacArthur Stadium and hit off the tee prior to the 12:30 contest.

Shortly after rising from his Ramada Inn bed, Mordecai's agenda was interrupted by a phone call.

"Hey, how you doing?" said the caller, Grady Little.

"I'm doing OK," Mordecai answered, a little confused. "How are you?"

"I'm not doing as good as you are, because you're going to the big leagues!"

Mordecai stood stunned in the middle of the hotel room. He knew that Little was not playing some cruel trick, not on such an important matter as the realization of a dream. For five-plus years in the minors, when others had viewed him as little more than a jack-of-all trades, master of none, when scouts had reported that he can't hit, can't throw and can't run, the 26-year-old Mordecai had continued to battle without complaining. Through it all, Little had been his biggest fan.

"I finally told Grady that was the greatest news I had ever heard," Mordecai said. "He was excited for me. I've played for Grady for four years. I think he's always been a guy who pulled for me and has been in my corner because I play hard and he knows that. He knows that when I go out to play, I don't do anything half-ass. I do everything full speed and I think he appreciates that because that's a reflection of your manager.

"But that phone call, that's a moment I'll always remember. You always wait on it, but you never know what it's going to feel like until it finally happens. It's a moment I won't forget."

Little's call to Mordecai occurred after Atlanta starting shortstop Jeff Blauser had to be placed on the 15-day disabled list because of a strained left oblique muscle. Blauser's backup, Rafael Belliard, was slated to join the lineup, with Mordecai taking over the reserve role. Mordecai hastily gathered his belongings, called his wife, Susie, with the best present she could receive on her twenty-third birthday, then went to the Syracuse airport and flew first-class to the major leagues.

Mike Mordecai survived life in the minors to get his taste of the major leagues. (Photo courtesy of Richmond Braves)

Once in Atlanta, it did not take Mordecai long to discover how plush life in the major leagues actually is. The Braves footed the bill for the rookie to stay at the Marriott Marquis for seven days. They also sprang for meal money, sixty dollars and fifty cents a day. Adding to the thrill was the fact that his parents could see his first appearances in the majors. They live in Birmingham, a two-hour trip along Interstate 20 from Atlanta. When Susie arrived after driving all day from Richmond, Mordecai felt as if he had the world by the tail.

"Mike Birkbeck calls making the majors 'six and six'," Mordecai said as he shook hands with new teammates outside his locker in the Atlanta clubhouse. "You make about six hundred dollars a day in salary, and you get about six hundred dollars in licensing money. To me, if I wasn't making any more money it would still be worthwhile to get a chance to play here."

Mordecai knew what it was like to be short of funds. Throughout his days in the minors, life was often a hand-to-mouth existence, not just for him, but for most players. One particular incident took place during his first season, 1989, in the Class A Midwest League. The Burlington Braves were winding up a road trip, and most of the players had already depleted their eleven dollars-a-day meal money, which had been doled to each player in one lump sum at the beginning of the trip. Trying to get as much to eat as possible, Mordecai and a teammate decided to share one plate at a Mexican restaurant.

"I'll keep the other guy anonymous, because neither one of us are proud of what took place," Mordecai said. "The people beside us left a rather large tip. The guy I was with looked over at me, got up, and took it off the table and paid for our meal with the tip. I really didn't want to have any part of it. But that's what some guys are forced to do when you're young, away from home and out of money."

Another money-related incident happened in June 1992, immediately after Mordecai had been promoted from Greenville to Richmond. Susie was living the nomadic life with her husband during the season instead of remaining alone at their permanent home near Birmingham. That meant Mordecai could not take over the lease agreement of the single player he was replacing on the Richmond roster. Instead, the Mordecais had to find living arrangements fast, because the R-Braves were leaving on a road trip in a couple of days.

Apartment-hunting was made more difficult by the rules surrounding a player's promotion from one level to the next. In order to receive an increase in pay, a player must spend 60 consecutive days at a club of higher classification. Mordecai, therefore, was still going to receive paychecks of $1,300 a month gross, the Double-A salary, instead of the Triple-A minimum of $1,700. Living arrangements in Richmond are significantly more expensive than the housing situation in Greenville, thereby leaving the city's newest residents limited in their options.

"Every apartment in Richmond was near about my whole salary," Mordecai said. "We looked around and wound up finding a place not far from the stadium. It was this little studio apartment where the bed folded out of the wall. We had a hole through the ceiling in the bathroom, where the shower was. You could see right through the roof of the house. My wife went out and bought some shower shoes because she wouldn't get in the shower in her bare feet. The whole thing was pretty bad."

Two other aspects made the situation more trying. Susie had just undergone surgery to remove a cyst from her hand, and was still feeling the effects of the anesthesia. Plus, the cabinets and refrigerator in the apartment's kitchen were empty, and the Mordecais had $23 in cash between them. The R-Braves were leaving for seven days, meaning Susie would be left in a strange place in a strange town with little money.

In trying times, one's faith can often play a significant role in the outcome. For the second time in his baseball career, Mordecai's membership in the Church of Christ proved especially beneficial. A minister in their Alabama congregation was friends with a contemporary in Richmond. Before the R-Braves had departed, Susie was in good hands.

"Susie called and they said, 'Don't worry about anything. We'll take care of you,'" Mordecai said. "They let her come over and do laundry at the house and fed her dinner. Everything worked out great."

Mordecai had been the recipient of similar attention while he played in Durham in 1990 and 1991. He and teammate Nate Minchey, also a member of the church, were searching for a place to stay the first season when they met

Bill and Margaret Weatherly. With two spare bedrooms, the Weatherlys offered the young players shelter, rent-free. Despite the houseguests pleas, the owners refused to accept any money. Four years later, Mordecai considered the Weatherlys as a second set of parents.

"They're like family now," Mordecai said. "That's just the type of people they are. They said, 'You guys are away from home. Spend your money when you call your family and take care of them as much as you can.' I tell you what, it sure made those two seasons a lot easier."

Mordecai appreciated such gestures, for he grew up in a household that exuded generosity and love. While money was available to pay the mortgage and put food on the table, his parents, Mike and Linda, had to work for everything they had. His father, a mechanic, was the breadwinner, and his mother had several jobs that made life a little easier.

"One of the reasons I'd like to stay in the big leagues is I'd love to be able to repay my parents for all they've done for me," Mordecai said. "I remember one job my mom had. She worked at a sporting goods store. My brother and I had all the best gloves and shoes, anything we needed for baseball. There were times when payday rolled around and the store would simply keep her check. She'd sometimes have to give them money for all the stuff she had gotten us. It's those kinds of things that make you want to earn some money and get them some things that they sacrificed for me."

The Mordecais supported their son's desire to play baseball, always attending practices and games and providing whatever assistance that was needed. Mike Sr. played on a local adult baseball team, and when his eldest son was just a toddler, he wanted a uniform to match his father's. From there, Mordecai's love for the game intensified. He gave up football his senior year of high school, even though several colleges were recruiting him to play on the gridiron. Instead, he wanted to provide himself with every opportunity to succeed on the diamond.

Pittsburgh was interested enough in Mordecai's services to draft him in the 33rd round after he graduated from Hewitt Trussville High School in 1986. Although playing professional baseball would be the beginning of a dream, Mordecai decided to hone his talents at the University of South Alabama. Three years later, his name was called by the Braves in the sixth round of the 1989 draft. Mordecai signed a contract and proceeded to hit .253 with 22 RBIs in 65 games at Burlington.

Anxious to see their son in a professional uniform, his parents traveled to Iowa to see Burlington's final series of the season. They took in the first two games against Hamilton before the team's trainer knocked on Mordecai's apartment door. He told Mordecai to pack his bags and head for Greenville. The shortstop had just been promoted for the Southern League playoffs.

"My parents drove back to Birmingham, but it wasn't that bad for them," Mordecai said. "Greenville and Birmingham both won the first round of the playoffs, so the two teams met for the championship and my parents got to see me when Greenville played the Barons in Birmingham."

Mordecai spent the next two seasons in Durham, hitting .280 in 72 games in 1990 and a team-high .262 the following year. He then opened the 1992 campaign in Greenville, batting .261, before joining Richmond on June 19 and finishing the season with a .246 norm. In 1993, he served most of the season by watching the prospect-laden Richmond club from the sidelines, although his ability to play anywhere on the field enabled him to see action in 72 contests, when he batted .268.

Through those five seasons, Mordecai never earned a reputation of anything more than a lukewarm major-league prospect. He had done every job asked of him, none to the extent that left the Braves drooling in anticipation. He had become a role player, one who would do whatever it took without complaining.

Some of those feelings had changed in the first month of the 1994 campaign, however. Mordecai took full advantage of receiving his first opportunity in nearly two seasons to play every day. The starting shortstop's defense was flawless, and his bat was producing at an unprecedented clip. His key hits had won several games for the R-Braves, among them a two-run, tie-breaking double in the eighth inning against Rochester on April 23. Mordecai's batting average was well above the .300 level, and his doubles total ranked among the International League leaders.

"One of the most important things to a season is getting off to a good start," Mordecai said. "If you can get off to a good start, especially when the weather's cold and it's hard to get in a groove, you're probably going to have a good season. It's no guarantee, but for a guy like me, I feel like I need to get off to a good start and just get things rolling.

"Now, a few weeks into it, here I am in the majors. I was just fortunate that things were going my way at the start of the year. I was doing well, playing short every day in Richmond and they needed an extra player. I guess I was in the right spot at the right time."

Quiet like most rookies in the Atlanta clubhouse, Mordecai's trip to the majors was a little easier because he knew many of his teammates after having played with them in the minors. A few members of the coaching staff also knew and appreciated the rookie's abilities. Bobby Cox was the team's general manager when Atlanta drafted him in 1989. Third-base coach Jimy Williams served as a roving coach with the organization during the first half of 1990 and remembered four years later the impression Mordecai made.

"He's the type of player who'll take ground balls and work until the bell rings," Williams said. "It's not a show. He's that dedicated to what he's doing. Some guys stand out due to their work ethic, and Mike's one of those. It all starts from the way they were raised. They're team players. They share and work well with other people. It just reinforces your belief in this game when you see a guy like him get a shot up here and get rewarded for his work."

Mordecai's shot, resembling ones most young players receive when serving a short-term reserve role, was limited in his first week with Atlanta. He did not see game action until May 9, taking a major-league field for the first time as a defensive replacement in the ninth inning of the Braves' 7-2 win over Philadelphia. He was back at shortstop late in the contest a night later, with Atlanta on the wrong end of an 8-1 score with the Phillies. Unsuccessful in his first major-league at bat in the eighth, he unexpectedly received another chance with the lumber an inning later, after the Braves had strung together five consecutive singles.

Atlanta-Fulton County Stadium was nearly empty when Mordecai walked to the plate. Even the shortstop's parents were back in Birmingham after attending the first few games of the homestand. With two runners on base, veteran pitcher Doug Jones stood on the mound, determined to stave off the home team's rally. He started the young hitter with a couple of palmballs, the last of which Mordecai clubbed hard but foul down the left-field line.

Mordecai stepped out of the right side of the batter's box, adjusted his gloves and thought about the situation as he took a deep breath. Time to look for something else, he figured, maybe a fastball. If it was an off-speed pitch, he could possibly adjust and make contact if he was looking for heat. However, if he was looking for a slower toss and got the cheese, chances are his swing wouldn't be able to catch up.

Back in the box, the 5-foot-10, 175-pound Mordecai gently swung his bat in front of him before cocking it at his right side. Jones reared back and unleashed the fastball. Mordecai was ready, his left leg striding forward. He wanted simply to make contact, possibly drill the ball back at the pitcher and up the middle. He instead got in front of the pitch ever so slightly, and the ball took off. When it landed over the outfield wall, a three-run homer in his second major-league at bat and his first hit in the Show, Mordecai had pulled the Braves within a run, at 8-7.

"I didn't even feel it," Mordecai said afterwards. "I just looked up and saw it going up. I don't even remember touching first base. If they had appealed the play at first, I don't know if I would have been called out or not."

Mordecai did indeed touch first. He then played impeccably in the field after Deion Sanders scored the tying run in the ninth on Javy Lopez's dribbler past first base. More than two hours and nearly six innings after Mordecai's heroics, the Braves won the game, 9-8, sixteen minutes after midnight. For Mordecai, the night was still young.

"I called my parents and talked to them for about an hour," Mordecai said the next morning. "I got to bed about three. Then I had to be back here at the stadium about eight. But if I could do this every day, I'd settle for three hours' sleep every night."

The thrills continued for Mordecai in the hours prior to the 12:30 game. A photographer from Topps, the same company that produced the baseball cards Mordecai used to collect as a kid, requested that the rookie pose for his first major-league card. Attired in his lily-white Braves uniform and holding the black bat he hit the home run with the previous evening, Mordecai was in the midst of experiencing everything he had always dreamed of doing.

"That's an even bigger thrill, getting my first baseball card picture," Mordecai said. "As for this bat, I got it last year, but I'd been saving it for a special occasion. Now it's going to be put up. I'm retiring it after last night."

Mordecai spent nine more days in the majors before returning to the R-Braves when Blauser came off the disabled list. He hardly moved off the bench after his May 10 contributions, yet Mordecai soon felt like a larger part of the team because of a couple initiation-type episodes. The first one took place following the final game of the homestand. The players were dressing in the clubhouse, preparing for the charter flight to Cincinnati, when Mordecai looked in his locker and discovered his suit and shoes had been pilfered. Hanging in their place was a red, pin-striped jacket, a red tie with stars, red pants and a pair of white, high-heeled shoes. With little time left before the bus departed for the airport, the rookie had no choice but to wear the new-found digs.

Once in Cincinnati, he along with fellow rookie Tony Tarasco were targeted for a prank that Reds visiting clubhouse manager Ernie Britton performs for every team. Britton brought out a metal cage, containing a mesh top and pretended to be feeding an animal inside it. The veterans gathered around, trying to lure either Tarasco or Mordecai. Mordecai was leery, but Tarasco took the bait. When the rookie outfielder got near the front of the cage, Britton pulled a string, causing the cage door to spring open and a furry tail to fly out. Tarasco nearly injured himself while screaming and jumping out of the way.

The event created much laughter for the next several days, proving once again why major-league baseball is often referred to as men playing a boys' game.

When Mordecai's 17-day ride in the majors concluded on May 20, he returned to a Richmond team that had dropped 11 of the 18 games it had played during the shortstop's absence. Many of the struggles could be blamed on a shakeup with the team's roster. A day after Mordecai was promoted to Atlanta, outfielder Mike Kelly was sent down to Richmond and Jarvis Brown was called up. Kelly, a highly touted flycatcher who was the team's first-round draft pick in 1991, had seen little action during his month in the majors, hitting just .185 in 26 at bats. The Atlanta brass felt a player of Kelly's caliber should be playing regularly instead of rusting away on the bench. Brown, considered a journeyman with little long-term value to the organization, was deemed better-suited in Atlanta than Kelly.

The rust was apparent during Kelly's first two weeks in Richmond. After joining the team in Ottawa, following an airline trip from hell that took him from Richmond to New York City to Albany, New York, to Canada, the outfielder had done little more than air-condition International League ballparks with his monstrous cuts, most of which had failed to make contact with the baseball. Through May 17, he was mired in a 1-for-28 slump, with 10 of his failures coming as strikeouts.

Injuries to two members of the pitching staff did not help matters. Dera Clark was placed on the disabled list May 15 with some fraying in the lining of the shoulder socket in his pitching arm, an ailment that shelved him for the remainder of the season. Two days later, the worst that had been feared regarding Mike Hostetler was now reality. The right-hander, who seemed on the verge of making a bid for the majors only a year earlier, would also miss the rest of the campaign because of the surgery required on his right elbow.

In the days prior to the departures of Clark and Hostetler, Little found himself in the unenviable position of being shorthanded. The situation climaxed on May 13 during a doubleheader with Scranton/Wilkes-Barre. When the first game reached the end of the 14th inning, Little had no one left in the bullpen. He asked for volunteers, and outfielder Brian Kowitz, who had not taken the mound since 1987 when he was in high school, offered his services.

The southpaw employed a slip-pitch, a toss the father of teammate Brian Bark had taught Kowitz. It was effective enough to limit the Red Barons to six hits and just one run. Kowitz then responded in the bottom of the 17th frame by leading off with a single before scoring on Jose Olmeda's triple. Intentional walks to Ed Giovanola and Kelly followed, setting the stage for Luis Lopez's game-winning single.

"I kind of got excited when Grady asked if anyone wanted to pitch," said Kowitz, who owned a 1-0 record and a 3.00 ERA in addition to a .290 batting average. "It's fun any time you can do something different. I was surprised I had the control I had. The only walk I had was an intentional one. I never imagined pitching three innings."

Anthony Telford saved the day for the Richmond staff in the second game. The veteran went the distance in a contest that took only an hour, 31 minutes. Taking nothing away from Telford's performance, but the Red Barons were probably wanting to leave The Diamond. The final out was recorded a minute after one that morning, less than 3½ hours before the team's wakeup call to return home to open a series with Ottawa.

Since that doubleheader sweep, the R-Braves had won just once in five contests entering the final game at Charlotte, an afternoon tilt. Little is typically in high spirits when he returns to "The Queen City." He lived in the city as a child, managed the Double-A team in the early 1980s, and was in the process of building a house in Pinehurst, about an hour-and-a-half drive away. Mired in the season's longest losing streak to date, combined with a couple of roster moves the skipper was none too happy with, left Little uncharacteristically perturbed.

Gregg Olson was not helping Little's mood. The pitcher was sent to Richmond on a 30-day rehabilitation assignment, bringing with him a major-league attitude. That trait was generally not present on Little's teams, especially this 1994 edition. In his short time with the club, Olson had done several irritating, undermining things. Little finally had enough. When Olson did not wear a tie as required of all players on plane trips, Little got in the pitcher's face and forced him to buy one at the airport and don it. Olson snapped back, but Little won the battle.

The final thing that got in Little's craw was the pitcher he received to replace Hostetler on the roster. The manager was expecting Brad Hassinger, a right-hander who was pitching well in Greenville. A uniform bearing Hassinger's name was even hanging in the visiting clubhouse of Knight's Castle. Instead, Don Strange was summoned from Laredo in the Mexican League. Having played for Little the previous two years, Strange was far from a favorite of the manager's. In fact, Strange's surname perfectly defined the right-hander. Many Richmond players called him "Stinky," primarily because the pitcher had not showered after games during spring training.

The situation caused Little to call a team meeting on the left-field lawn at 11:30, an hour prior to the game with Charlotte. It was more a pep talk than a tongue-lashing, although the manager got his point across with a combination of a few well-placed barbs and direct hits. The pow-wow had little immediate effect; the R-Braves dropped their fifth straight, 4-2 to the Knights. Long-term, however, the results would be seen, for everyone knew where everything stood.

"Grady's a good guy to play for," said Mike Birkbeck, sitting at the far end of the Richmond dugout after the meeting. "Grady's the type of guy, he doesn't say much a lot of the time, but he knows what's happening. Day to day he's pretty quiet. That's what scares you about him."

Birkbeck grinned after that final comment, one of the few things that had given the right-hander reason to smile in the last two weeks. He began the season with 11 scoreless innings and 13 strikeouts in his first two starts, but left his April 30 game after $2^{2}/_{3}$ innings because of a strained muscle in his right knee. Two starts later, Birkbeck was uncharacteristically touched for six runs in six innings. An indication of how rare that was could be seen in Birkbeck's numbers since the beginning of the 1993 campaign. In 28 starts he surrendered more than four runs only four times, and had not allowed more than three earned runs or seven hits in his first six starts of 1994.

His streak of atypical performances continued in the first game of the Charlotte series on May 16. Refusing to give in to his aching knee or to a groin that continued to tighten with the consistency of a boa constrictor, Birkbeck kept Richmond in the game by hurling six innings, allowing three earned runs, seven hits and striking out six. Nevertheless, he was as much a warrior as a pitcher, resulting in a 2-2 record and an uncommonly high but decent 3.63 ERA.

He would never admit it, but Birkbeck's efforts provided some needed leadership-by-example for the R-Braves, a trait rarely seen by a 33-year-old pitcher trying to scratch and claw his way back to the majors. Others in his position would be more like Olson, whose self-centered attitude indicated he felt the Triple-A level was beneath him. And while no one would describe Birkbeck as a rah-rah player, he quietly went about his business while helping younger teammates with any problems they may have.

"I don't try to be a leader here," Birkbeck said. "I just try to do my job, put a good day's work in, and get better. Whatever my responsibility is that day, I try to do it the best I can. If it's with the radar gun and chart or if I go out there on the mound, I try to do it the best that I can, because I am getting paid.

"I remember in Milwaukee, we were in the race most of the time I was there, but one year we were out of it. I remember one of the older guys was saying he was still getting paid over a 162-game schedule. That's the way it is here. If I wasn't getting paid, I might not care. But it's my job."

Speculation had increased in recent weeks as to which Richmond pitcher would have his responsibilities include a start for Atlanta. The Braves were

Mike Birkbeck made his mark by quietly leading by example. (Photo courtesy of Richmond Braves)

rained out during back-to-back contests in St. Louis, games that were to be made up as doubleheaders in late July. That scenario would have the two teams square off six times in four days, meaning at least one minor-league hurler would have to be brought in for a day. Given his production over the past year and a half and his experience at the game's top level, Birkbeck was considered the logical candidate.

"Why would they call me?" Birkbeck responded. "They got long relievers they'll go with. They don't care what I'm doing. They never ask me. Anyway, if I start thinking about that, it'll just affect what I'm trying to do here."

Asked if he was trying to get back to the majors by pitching in Richmond, Birkbeck smirked as he looked out of the corners of his dark brown eyes. "With Atlanta?" his facial expression seemed to say. Yeah, right.

Roster Moves

10

Richmond was not the only team in the organization experiencing difficulties during the early stages of May. The chain reaction caused by Mike Mordecai's promotion and a handful of injuries created a riptide of losses, from the top rungs of the ladder down to the bottom.

Greenville posted victories in just two of its first 11 games in the season's second month, and had dropped 12 of 15 dating back to the final days of April. Some players began to wonder if a worse team had been seen by their observers. But the situation, while dismal during a six-game losing skein that ended May 11 on Jason Schmidt's third win of the year, was far from terminal.

"We've had one good streak so far and one bad one," said Bruce Benedict, who was handling the losses much better as Greenville's manager than some predicted. "We ran into a couple hot clubs. Then it seemed like we got into a deal where on nights we got good pitching, we didn't score, and nights where we hit, we couldn't get anybody out. We've gotten into a little bit of a rut in those areas.

"We also got hurt by a couple of injuries. We lost our starting shortstop, Hector Roa, with a broken thumb. And Ed Giovanola went to Triple-A because Mordecai went to the big leagues. It's taken us a few days to try to adjust to Ed's loss because he was a real stabilizer for us, both on and off the field. He and Tim Gillis are the type of guys who really help our club because our starting pitchers are young and inexperienced. When you lose a veteran guy, it hurts."

In place of Roa, the most universally detested player in the organization, the G-Braves received shortstop Jason Keeline, a weak-hitting infielder who instantly improved the up-the-middle defense for the team. As for the departure of Giovanola, who would remain and succeed in Richmond for the remainder of the campaign, Greenville was handed Kevin Grijak, Durham's player of the month for April after hitting .368 with 11 home runs in 22 games.

Grijak rocketed to the best offensive start in the organization. Roving catching instructor Joe Szekely jokingly asked the Durham coaching staff during one early May visit what they were feeding the first baseman/ outfielder. After all, he had gone deep just 22 times in his first three minor-league seasons. Ironically, Szekely's question was not far from the mark.

"I've been taking my vitamins and eating a well-balanced diet," Grijak said. "I go grocery shopping. Before, it was strictly Wendy's and McDonald's, and that's not really good for a professional athlete. You've got to have your carbohydrates and proteins to remain healthy and play your best.

"I also finally adapted to getting myself ready for a game and all that goes with it. I wanted to come out here with a vengeance, just go out with authority and really kick some ass. And it's paying off. I'm starting to mature as a professional, and I'm starting to realize that when you go about your business on and off the field, good things will happen. I've been really conscientious about my lifestyle, the eating habits and sleeping habits. Getting my proper rest really determines how you're going to perform. It might not happen just one day, but it's going to end up taking its toll later in the year if you mess around a little bit. Everything has been paying dividends."

Prior to the 1994 season, Grijak's claim to fame had been earning first-team All-Mid-American Conference accolades while at Eastern Michigan University. He had always been a capable hitter since the Braves selected him with their 29th pick in the 1991 draft, batting .337 with 10 homers and 58 RBIs at Idaho Falls in 1991 and ranking 10th in the South Atlantic League in 1993 with a .296 batting average. His defense was less than stellar, thereby limiting his consideration as a prospect.

"Kevin is a dichotomy in the sense that he's a 23-, almost 24-year-old position player who started the year in high A ball," said Matt West. "If you counted the number of guys in the major leagues who were playing A ball at that age, you wouldn't get many. But then again, it looks like to me that Kevin has the possibility to be that late bloomer. The organization feels very highly about his hitting skills. If he is able to do the things defensively that we're trying to get him to do, he might be a prospect. You can't ignore the fact that he has tremendous potential at the plate."

Peering through his ice-blue eyes, Grijak seemed unaffected by the game that takes place off the field. As long as his name was on the lineup card on a regular basis, he seemed content to let the game and the subsequent politics run their course.

"Ever since I signed, I've said to myself, 'This is some fun stuff out here,'" Grijak said. "I've been fortunate to get drafted and play professionally. That was my ultimate goal. Now that it's happened, I've been taking strides just to get to where I am right now. And no matter how old you are or what weaknesses you have, as long as you go out there and prove to them you can play, you can go a long way in this game."

It did not take much time for one of Grijak's weaknesses to come to the forefront at the Double-A level. Manning first base in his first game with the G-Braves, Grijak let a routine ground ball in the ninth inning at Nashville roll under his glove and set the stage for the winning run. As a result, closer Brad Clontz suffered his first loss and first blown save of the year after succeeding in his first 11 chances. In fact, that would be the only save opportunity Clontz would not wrap up before receiving a promotion to Richmond on July 14.

Grijak's bat, however, was a welcome addition to the punchless G-Braves' offense, which was shut out five times in May. A week after his promotion, he won a game in the bottom of the ninth with a single against Huntsville. The team, meanwhile, eventually slipped five games under the break-even mark after a 4-3 loss at Carolina on May 23, then regrouped at the end of the month by winning six of its last eight games.

"I think our weak points have been any sort of consistent offense," Benedict said as his G-Braves entered June in second place with a 27-28 record. "Early on we were getting timely hits. I knew that wasn't going to last, where you get that big hit every time you need it. But we have the ability to score some runs. Plus, I think when you have a young team and young pitching, you expect to struggle a little bit early in the year until they make their adjustments and settle down. It's a tough league."

Greenville's gain in Grijak was Durham's loss, and the absence of his stick was consequential. The month had been arduous even prior to Grijak's May 10 promotion, with the Bulls dropping all but two of their first nine games. After an 8-6 stretch, West's team again hit the skids, dropping six of its last seven contests to end the month 10-18.

Unlike Benedict, West had difficulty with defeat. His intense personality became so tightly wound that observers expected something to pop, whether it would be one of the veins in the manager's forehead or one of the baseballs he angrily threw in batting practice. Even such small talk as "How's it going?" drew West's wrath.

"How the f--- do you think it's going?" West sardonically responded to a visitor's greeting. "That's a pretty obvious answer." The manager looked over at his batting coach, Rick Albert, rolled his eyes, then walked out of the dugout during pregame drills.

West was also having to cope with a juggled roster after experiencing few changes during the season's first month. The Bulls lost Keeline to Greenville on May 4, then struggled at the shortstop position when his replacement, Julio

Trapaga, was placed on the disabled list with a strained groin. Atlanta responded by sending Keeline back to Durham, only to have the 25-year-old decide enough was enough. He retired from baseball, opting to return home to California and begin the next phase of his life.

Keeline's retirement surprised many of his teammates. Signed as an undrafted free agent in 1991, he was in the midst of putting together his best season. While he batted just .154 during 14 games with the Bulls, Keeline responded to the challenge of the Double-A level by hitting .290 with four RBIs in 10 outings with the G-Braves. His defense was as good as any shortstop the organization had to offer at either Greenville or Durham, and his attitude was professional and determined.

Yet, deep down, Keeline seethed over the way he felt he was treated by the organization. He watched angrily as roving instructors helped other players while failing to even conjure up a "hello" to Keeline before leaving town. His frustration reached a boiling point toward the end of the 1993 season during a postgame picnic held by the Macon booster club. Keeline approached roving hitting coach Jay Ward, who was adamant about following orders and working only with prospects. Said the shortstop, "Those guys aren't the only ones who need help. Punch-and-Judy hitters like me could use some help, too." So stunned was Ward that he had a hard time responding after nearly choking on his mouthful of food.

The organization was also a little surprised about Keeline's departure. "I always pulled for Jason and tried to watch out for him," said Bobby Dews. "He was a good-field, no-hit middle infielder, just like I was. I thought I saw some of myself in him. He was the kind of defensive player you need in an organization. Most guys can field the ball. Hell, some guys could wake up out of a dead sleep after having 10 drinks on Christmas Eve and field ground balls. But the question is, can they do it on a hard-hit grounder with the score tied and the winning run on third in the bottom of the ninth? It takes a special player to do that every time. Teams need those kinds of guys.

"I know it's a cliche, but as long as you have that uniform on your back, you have a chance. Baseball is full of hope; that's all the game is at this level. But if you don't have hope, you don't have anything. It's the guys that just wear you down and refuse to quit that succeed. Take a guy like Mike Mordecai. He kept fighting until he finally got a shot. And look what happened! Jason, on the other hand, hit .290 in Double-A and got mad about being sent down. Hitting .300 is no big deal. I'm afraid his decision told us something about him."

The Bulls were soon without another teammate, only this was not at the player's request. Left-handed pitcher Jason Butler, one of the more popular members of the Bulls' roster, became the first player West had to release as a manager. Butler had struggled as a starter and as a reliever since signing as an undrafted free agent out of Southeastern Illinois College in 1991. In 1994, his control abandoned him, resulting in 18 walks in 27 innings and a 2-2 record with a 5.93 ERA. Everyone knew Butler had been not effective, yet his release sent shockwaves through the clubhouse.

"Jason had to be the nicest guy you could ever meet," said pitcher Ken Giard. "When we heard the news, you said that if it was somebody else, you'd feel bad. But with Jason, it's really a sad moment.

"It also makes you realize how lucky you are to have a uniform. I feel very lucky. This is my fourth year and I'm hoping to play a lot longer. I'm just hoping to keep on going."

Releasing a player is generally one of the hardest chores a manager must handle. The skipper is, in essence, telling a young man that his dreams are no longer realistic, at least in the opinion of that organization. As Chuck LaMar preaches to the minor-leaguers every spring, "We're not running a YMCA around here." An organization must see improvement in order to justify the roster spot. If that does not take place, then it is almost always best for everyone involved to go his separate way and search for other options.

West, predictably, showed little outward emotion a day after cutting the heart out of Butler's dreams. "I guess it's tough, but for a guy like Jason, it's the best thing for him," said the skipper. "If he wants to keep going, then maybe he can catch on and have a better situation for him somewhere else. Otherwise he can get on with his life. You start every season wanting to coach the same guys until they move up. It's hard to release or send a guy down. But that's life in baseball."

As for the remaining players on the roster, a couple pitchers were showing improvement. Most notably was Mike D'Andrea, who stood at 3-4 with a team-low ERA of 4.29, though the results were still far from satisfactory. Matt Murray was just 3-6 with a 4.82 ERA in 11 starts. Jamie Arnold was even more erratic, posting a 4-4 record and a 4.95 ERA in 11 openings. Arnold had also surrendered 11 home runs and walked as many batters as he had struck out — 35.

The situation was similarly inconsistent with the offense. Other than designated hitter Mike Warner, who was hitting a team-high .311 after coming off the disabled list May 13, few batters could find a groove. After entering the month on one of the Carolina League's hottest streaks, Tom Waldrop had hit safely in just six of his last 53 trips to the plate, and had seen his batting average plummet from a high of .293 to its current .219. Catcher Brad Rippelmeyer was not faring much better, recording six hits in his last 51 at bats, and was batting a mere .211. With those kinds of numbers, there was little wonder why Durham had not won more than two consecutive games during the first two months of the season.

Losing was not a new sensation in Macon, either. The daily grind that produced a 3-23 record in April and losses in eight of the first 10 games in May did little to numb the sting. Frustration was the common denominator on the club. Incredibly, the players were displaying an uncanny ability of sticking together in their efforts to reverse the course.

"I'm not complaining, but we're not on the same page with a lot of clubs in this league," Rod Gilbreath said while watching infield practice in early May. "We have a high school-oriented draft, and other teams are putting college kids in their second and third (professional) years here. Those guys are 23, 24, 25 years old. A 25-year-old player ought to be in the majors, not the Sally League. What there needs to be is age limits. There are rookie and experience levels, but that doesn't mean a thing.

"We're going to be fine. If we can get a guy or two to Greenville next year and have them skip a level, we've done our job. If we can promote half the roster to Durham next year, we've done our job. While we want to win games, wins and losses are not that important. We're in the business of developing talent, developing baseball players. And if we do that, we've been successful. It may not look like it now, but we're going to be fine here once July and August roll around."

If any encouraging sign was present, it came in the fact that rarely was Macon getting blown out. Other teams were taking advantage of scoring opportunities, while the Braves were letting similar situations slip through their gloves and roll through their legs.

An example came in a 6-4 loss to Savannah on May 5. After leading off the fourth inning with a strikeout that culminated with a 95 mile-per-hour fastball that emulated an aspirin, Macon's Jason Green surrendered a double on his following pitch. Knowing that he had to keep the ball down in order to be successful, Green quickly overcompensated by walking the next two batters, with most of the pitches bouncing at least two feet in front of the plate. Leon Roberts had seen enough at that point, and opted to go with Ryan Jacobs out of the bullpen.

Upon entering the game with the bases juiced, Jacobs allowed one run to score when he walked the first batter on four pitches. Jason Birdlinger then ripped an ant-killer up the middle, driving in two more runs, giving the visitors a 4-0 lead.

In Macon's half of the inning, catcher Sean Smith led off with a two-bagger to left-center, yet was still at second base when the frame ended. Jermaine Dye lofted a weak can of corn to left, Wonderful Monds fanned badly on a curveball that was at least three feet outside and John Knott struck out on a fastball that was up around his eyes.

"They're just not picking up things as fast as they need to," Leon Roberts said a couple days later. "We're making many more mental errors than we should. The physical errors are fine if you're hustling. But the mental ones, there's no excuse. That's what we have to correct."

The echoes of Roberts' assessment were still audible on Friday, the 13th of May, when without notice, Macon began to receive a dash of good fortune. Behind three hits and four runs batted in by Dye, the Braves equalled a season-high for runs in topping the RiverDogs, 10-5, in Charleston. A 7-1 victory over Charleston followed on Saturday before Carey Paige tossed a three-hitter over $7^{2}/_{3}$ innings to guide the Braves to a 2-1 triumph and Macon's first three-game winning streak of the year.

The Braves won their fourth in a row a night later at Luther Williams Field when they came from behind to beat Charleston, 6-5, then made it five straight after Knott got Macon on the board early with a three-run homer in the first inning of the team's 5-1 win over Fayetteville. The Generals gained revenge with a 13-3 decision on May 18, but Macon refused to retreat and came back to win 7-6 on Thursday.

In seven days' time, Macon showed a level of maturity that had been missing for the first five weeks of the season. And it continued. The Braves came out on top in six of their last 11 games of the month to conclude May with a 14-14 record, 17-37 overall. Those efforts may not have created any trembles throughout the league, but it did prove that the early-season comments by LaMar, Gilbreath and Roberts could indeed turn out to be prophetic.

"It's going better than it was, that's for sure," Knott said. "But that doesn't make it any better..."

Such "me first" comments, where the frustration poured out of Knott as rapidly as the sweat from his body in the 94-degree heat, were why the third baseman had become somewhat of an outsider on the Macon team. He put himself in the position at the beginning of the season by pouting about his desire to be in Durham. And while he had emerged as one of the more consistent offensive forces in the lineup, Knott continued to dwell on what could have been instead of what was taking place.

"I want to get up there to Durham," said Knott, who saw his batting average increase to .239 by late May. "I have no idea what the front office wants me to do. If they want me to hit more home runs, I'll hit more home runs. If they want me to hit for average, I'll hit for average. Same thing with stolen bases. But I don't know what they want 'cause they don't tell me anything."

Making matters worse for Knott were the telephone calls he and a few of his veteran teammates sporadically received from their pals toiling in Durham. The players shared notes, and those at Durham offered encouragement. Also slipped into the conversations was the electric atmosphere at The Dap. When Knott hung up and reported to Luther Williams Field and its 500 or so fans who had a hard time being heard over the sparrows that nested underneath the press box that hangs from the ballpark's roof, the third baseman simply became more depressed and agitated.

"At least we're beginning to win some games," Knott said as he swatted the swarm of gnats in the Macon dugout. "It doesn't get much worse than being here and losing. A few wins and a few hits definitely make it a little more tolerable."

Drafting Decisions

11

The telephone rang three times at the Hartsville, South Carolina, home before a middle-aged man answered.

"May I speak with Jacob Shumate?" asked the caller.

"I'm sorry, you don't have the right number."

"Would you happen to know a Jacob Shumate?"

"Oh, I figure just about everybody knows Jacob. I'm his uncle. Just a minute and I'll get his daddy's number for you."

The caller was speaking shortly thereafter with the desired Shumate, the same one who a few minutes earlier on the afternoon of June 2 had been selected 27th in the first round of the annual amateur draft by the Atlanta Braves.

"Everybody hopes for this to happen," said the young pitcher. He spoke with nervous excitement, yet was refreshingly naive about the waters he was dipping his toes into. "I was anxious this morning at graduation practice. I couldn't wait to get back home and see if someone would call."

When an 18-year-old can throw a fastball that moves and jumps as it travels more than 90 miles an hour over the course of about 60 feet, someone will notice, and someone will call. In fact, scouts representing every major-league team had observed the right-hander, beginning when he first took the mound for Hartsville High School three years earlier. He had since heard what every professional team and practically every major college program had to offer. A preliminary decision had been made for Shumate to attend the University of South Carolina on a combination baseball/football offer. However, with some serious money awaiting should he opt for the professional ranks, college was simply a bargaining chip.

By the end of the month, Shumate was a half-million dollars richer while wearing a Braves uniform in Danville, Virginia. The same held true for Atlanta's compensatory second-round choice, Corey Pointer, a high school catcher from Waxahachie, Texas, who reported to West Palm Beach after signing on the dotted line for two hundred grand.

The surprise of the draft came later in the second round, with the 61st pick overall. Atlanta selected outfielder George Lombard, considered by most college football recruiting services as the nation's best high school running back. His experience on the diamond consisted of approximately 35 games, yet a day after the draft he was preparing to head for Florida. The Braves and $425,000, the most money ever given to a second-round draft pick, had convinced the talented athlete that professional baseball offered much more in return than a shot at the Heisman Trophy at the University of Georgia.

"We gambled a little bit because of Lombard's signability," Chuck LaMar said. "He told everybody in baseball that it was going to take a first-round pick and a lot of money to sign him, and rightfully so. As we got closer to the draft, George let it be known to us that he truly wanted to play the game of baseball and wanted to be an Atlanta Brave. So we gambled that other clubs would back off of him because of his signability and his football commitment."

Lombard's signing was not unprecedented in Atlanta draft annals. Since teams select players in reverse order of their league standing at the end of the preceding season, the Braves had been left the last couple years with late first-round selections, a time when the cream of the crop had been picked over. The best remaining players were those with an asterisk. They either told teams not to bother due to college commitments or had priced themselves out of the market. With the Braves' charge to excellence and a healthy bank account, LaMar made the decision to work around the problems and gamble on signing the best talent available. As a result, Atlanta acquired the services of such perceived difficult signs as Jason Schmidt, Jamie Howard, Andre King and now George Lombard, thereby keeping the farm system loaded with talent despite less-than-advantageous draft positions.

Shumate, Pointer and Lombard represented the first three of 58 players the Braves selected during the three-day marathon that is professional baseball's draft. Unlike the sport's counterparts on the gridirons and hardwoods, the baseball draft is done via a conference call instead of in front of television cameras. Despite the lack of media attention, the draft is considered by many major-league organizations to be the most important three days of the entire year.

"It's a lot of work, but a lot of fun," LaMar said with a sparkle in his eye that only a fellow scout would understand. "This time of year is what it's all about. The month of May is when we're making final decisions on players, putting the final touches on players from area scouts on what they've done all year. The scouts have been away from their families, putting as many miles as possible on that car, all with the focus being on June second, third and fourth."

The Braves' scouting brass huddled in a suite at Atlanta's Omni International Hotel with a stack of index cards containing the names of more than 500 available players that represented thousands of hours of work. The work is often unscientific, for a scout must project how a teenager's body and talents will develop and mature over the next five or so years. His final projections are based on numerous criteria, ranging from the player's parents' physiques to a variety of mental, physical and psychological tests.

Compiling a draft list is also the culmination of efforts that could be as many as four years in the making. In the case of a talented youngster such as Shumate, either a part-time bird dog or an area scout will first notice him as a high school freshman or sophomore, usually while watching older players for previous drafts. Should the player continue to excel in the spring prior to his draft-eligible year, he will be observed by a team's area supervisor. Individual workouts, psychological exams, eye tests and meetings at the player's house with his parents will follow. If the player is deemed among the nation's elite, a regional supervisor will come to town, along with some of the team's top executives. Similar efforts take place with each of the nation's top draft-eligible players, resulting in a time figure that would be as overwhelming as the efforts are exhausting.

Beginning two weeks prior to the draft, LaMar meets with each of his 20 area supervisors and 15 United States scouts to go over the discovered players. Regional supervisors and national cross-checkers are then consulted before heading out the week prior to the draft for a final look. That type of effort leaves little doubt that the Braves do not hold the same beliefs as Cincinnati owner Marge Schott, who chopped her team's scouting department to the bare bones in recent years because, as she has said, "All scouts do is sit around and watch baseball games."

"The teams that are able to continue to spend the money that they need in scouting and player development will be the successful organizations over the long haul," LaMar said. "It's the life blood of every organization. That's sort of an overused term, but it's so very true."

The Braves' draft philosophy also differs from those of other teams in another way. A higher percentage of players have been drafted from college baseball than the high school classrooms since 1977. For the past 15 years, 52 percent of all first-round choices have college experience. In 1994, a total of 1,707 players were selected by the 28 major-league teams, with 54.4 percent of those coming from the college ranks.

Atlanta, conversely, prefers high school players, especially in the first 20 rounds. In doing so, the organization can mold the youngsters while their bodies are still maturing and before they reach their athletic peak. The players are taught the Braves' way of playing baseball without the need of deprogramming, as can be the case with college players.

College players offer several other challenges that high school players do not. Age is a primary concern. College players are typically three years older than their prep counterparts, meaning their time is limited in terms of making the necessary adjustments in the minors. The advanced age also means that many college players have reached their athletic peaks, and are as good as they are ever going to be.

High school players present one negative that causes cost-conscious teams to go the college route. Most top draftees have scholarships awaiting at major universities, where college coaches preach the value of an education and the broad experience they can offer. The coaches also harp on the statistics, among them the fact that just one in 10 of all drafted players ever reaches the majors for at least one game. Even first-round picks are no sure thing, with just 70 percent of those players in the 1980s reaching the Show.

Major-league teams counteract that argument by pointing to the advanced development gained by playing professional baseball on a daily basis. Add in the fact that college can be attended at any time in life, unlike the opportunity to play professional baseball, along with the enticement of a nice signing bonus, and a young player with the dream of reaching the majors has a hard time saying no to playing for pay.

All the attention and the subsequent decisions a young athlete faces makes the situation as draining and stressful as it is invigorating and gratifying. And for a first-round selection who decides to turn pro, those sensations are just the tip of the iceberg. Expectations from the team, family members and friends combined with the constant dime-store evaluations on his development by the media and fans has led to more than one burning sensation in the pit of a promising player's stomach.

One player to experience such sensations is Tyler Houston, Atlanta's first-round selection in 1989 and the second overall pick in the draft. A switch-hitting catcher with a plethora of skills, Houston was thought to be on a freight train to stardom after earning Gatorade West Region player-of-the-year honors following his senior season at Valley High School in Las Vegas. But since that time, his train derailed, leaving Houston to spin his wheels in frustration in the upper levels of the minor leagues.

Houston's defensive abilities have always been above standards despite his abnormal throwing mechanics. Yet, his failure to develop into a stellar power hitter and his disappointing .231 career batting average entering the 1994 season dominated all assessments and caused him to go from a prospect to a suspect seemingly overnight. He had enjoyed some success, walloping a 460-foot home run in his second pro at bat, maintaining strong production with 13 homers and 56 RBIs in 1991, and earning a spot on the Double-A All-Star team in 1993. Holding him back was his inability to reach the lofty goals established by others, which had led to five years of disappointment.

"When I first came out of high school, there were so many expectations," Houston said in an empty Richmond dugout before a June home game. "Everybody was riding my bandwagon. Then my first (full) year, I was a 19-year-old kid, hit 13 home runs and caught well that season. I just didn't hit for a good average. They started writing me off right there. As a 19-year-old, that's really hard. I don't think that's right to do to anybody. That can really ruin a kid's career. I think people need to realize that they're not dealing with men yet. They need to give the kids a chance."

Houston at times had been his own worst enemy. Adding to his plummeting stock was his reputation of having a bad attitude. On several occasions as a professional he has been thrown out of games in the middle of an at bat because of arguments with the home plate umpire about balls and strikes. Rarely does he interact with fellow members of the team, opting instead to march quietly to the beat of a different drummer. He has also gone through periods of refusing to speak to anyone with a microphone and pad, believing he would not get a fair shake even if he went out of his way to accommodate.

"If the press would just give you a chance," Houston continued. "A guy coming out of high school is naturally going to be a little green at the beginning. Then you kind of mature and you start to understand the role and understand about professional baseball and the minor leagues. What people don't understand is it's hard. It's a job. You travel, you're away from home. You immediately move out of your house and you're on the road all the time. Then dealing with the stress of the press and not playing well, it's hard on a kid. I don't envy any of the top-round picks coming out and not doing well right away."

Other elements in addition to baseball contributed to Houston's stress and inconsistent behavior. He came from a broken home and was raised during his high school days by his father, Sam Houston, a former Braves minor-leaguer in the 1970s. The elder Houston was an airline pilot who maintained two apartments due to his odd working hours, often leaving Tyler alone for long stretches. Tyler wound up having to face many events, including much of the hoopla surrounding the draft, by himself.

Shortly after signing with Atlanta, Houston married his high school sweetheart, only to divorce less than a year later. He continued to struggle with many aspects of his life until 1993, when he began to show some rejuvenated promise by batting .372 during the first two months at Greenville. He quickly succumbed to a June swoon, and hit just .208 the rest of the way before receiving a promotion to Richmond on August 18.

During the first two months of the 1994 season, the 23-year-old Houston split his time between first base and catcher at Richmond. His defense was still solid, and his bat continued to miss more often that not, resulting in a .226 average for a 31-25 team that, like Houston, refused to surrender until the final out was recorded. Houston was also continuing to mature, and the freight train, at least in terms of his personal life, was back on track. He married again, this time to Gabrielle, and seemed to have a grip on baseball instead of baseball handling him.

"Every year I go in with the attitude that it's a new season and it's a new start," Houston said. "I'm enjoying the game a lot more. I'm more relaxed. I finally learned to blank out all the pressure and all the other crap that gets in your head and just play. If something happens, it happens. If not, there's nothing I can do about it. I think I made the adjustments that are going to help me now."

Other first-round picks experience similar ups and downs. Two rungs down the organization ladder at Durham, Jamie Arnold has pitched inconsistently during his first two years with the Braves. He admits that sometimes the spotlight never seems to dim, although much of the attention from his teammates has diminished.

"I really don't feel any pressure," Arnold said. "I did when I first got drafted. I figured that everyone was watching me and that I had to do extra good. Now I realize that by this level, everybody's in the same boat. I don't think I'm better than anybody on my pitching staff. People who still acknowledge me as a first-round pick might like to think I'm a prima donna, but I don't try to act any better than anyone else. I just consider myself one of the guys. When I'm out there pitching, I feel like we have nine players on the field, and everybody can do his job and do it well or else they wouldn't be here."

Even with the unexpected adjustments and the subsequent hills and valleys the minors have offered Arnold the past two years, the pitcher believed he made the right decision to sign out of high school.

"I wouldn't change it for the world," Arnold said. "I think this is the best experience of my life. I had some doubts when I was going into the draft of whether or not to sign and play or to get my education over with. The way I looked at it is, this could be a once in a lifetime chance for me. I could've gone to college and ended up hurting myself and not ever getting this chance. I figured that even though college was important, I could always go back. If I hurt myself doing this, I wouldn't have to wonder if I could have made it or not. Now, if everything works out right, in a couple of years I hope to be fulfilling my dream in the major leagues."

The Braves' high school-oriented draft relieves the anxieties many minor-league players in other organizations experience around draft time. Mid to late June is often the time when many teams have traditionally dumped struggling players in favor of new draft choices. Since most of Atlanta's choices are so young, and with three rookie-league teams to place the newcomers, most veteran players in the full-season circuits do not have to worry about new blood taking their spots in the organization, at least not until next spring.

Turning the Paige

12

In most minor leagues below the Triple-A level, seasons are divided into equal halves, each consisting of about 70 games, with June 20 often serving as the dividing point. Teams in first place at midseason qualify for the playoffs in early September, while clubs with even the worst first-half records can rekindle some hope and start anew.

Midseason is also when the South Atlantic League hosts its annual all-star game. Although all-star recognition is always an honor to receive, players are not always thrilled with having an extra game to play. Most prefer to see baseball and the city in which they are playing quickly disappear in the rearview mirror. And that's exactly what many Macon Braves did late in the evening of June 18. The Macon clubhouse was empty within a half-hour of the team's hastily played victory over Albany that Saturday night. The players had begun drives as much as 14 hours in length to see girlfriends throughout the Southeast and Midwest. Such trips were nothing for young men who had endured wearisome bus trips for the past 2½ months, even if they had to be back in Macon by Tuesday.

Three Macon players did not have the luxury of a three-day vacation. Jermaine Dye, anointed the starting right fielder for the National League squad, pitcher Carey Paige, and outfielder Wonderful Monds, a late addition due to an injury to another player, piled in a car with a small Braves delegation and traveled more than 300 miles north to Hickory, North Carolina, site of the 1994 SAL All-Star Game.

Known as "America's Best-Balanced City" because of the strong presence of both furniture and textile manufacturing, Hickory has in the past decade become a hotbed for fiber optics production. But even that high-tech industry proved to be little more than a flicker compared to the interest the city of 25,000 had shown its baseball team since the beginning of the 1993 campaign. After being without professional baseball since the Rebels succumbed at the end of the 1960 season, Hickory residents embraced their Crawdads like a barbecue sandwich and a draft beer. The turnstiles at the red brick-and-concrete L.P. Frans Stadium clicked 283,727 times in 1993, the league's all-time high.

Hickory's success was not limited to attendance. Featuring one of the ever-growing unique names found in the minors and an equally creative logo, Crawdad souvenirs vaulted near the top of minor-league sales during the team's inaugural season. Thousands of caps, jerseys and T-shirts had been sold throughout the city as well as the country via the team's toll-free telephone number.

Success experienced by Hickory as well as such clubs as Durham, Carolina and Chattanooga created a revenue generator that was practically untapped by minor-league teams until the late 1980s. The Bulls were the first team to reap the rewards, caused by the demand created by the film *Bull Durham*. The Columbus Mudcats then stumbled into the arena in 1989 during a last-ditch effort to spawn some interest for a new stadium in the west Georgia city. In a rename-the-team contest, general manager Joe Kremer sorted through more than 500 different suggestions before coming across "Mudcats," a low-swimming fish that can be found aplenty in the Chattahoochee River, which runs across the street from the front gate of Columbus' Golden Park.

"We wanted either a positive or a negative reaction, we didn't care which," Kremer said. "We just wanted somebody to notice something was going on. We almost went with Scrambled Dogs, a glorified chili dog that's indigenous to the Columbus area. But we opted for Mudcats, which a lot of people did not like to start with."

Kremer, team president Steve Bryant and Frank Harrod, an artistically inclined friend of the two baseball men, sat down in a restaurant one winter evening and sketched some ideas on the back of cocktail napkins. A few strokes of ink produced a face-first, open-mouthed fish emerging from the letter "C". A slight alteration here and there followed before the minors' soon-to-be most popular logo was created.

By 1994, practically every team in the minors was heavily involved in souvenir sales. Teams that had long taken the name of their major-league affiliates were coming up with new monikers in order to cash in on the business. Others at least changed their logo, even if they kept their previous nickname. The Lookouts of Chattanooga brought in more than a half-million dollars after designing a rather simple logo, sporting a capital "C" with a pair of eyes bugging out of the middle, in 1991.

Among the few teams still employing names of their major-league affiliates were Macon, Greenville and Richmond. All three teams are owned by the Braves, and except for the caps, the players dress in uniforms exactly like the ones the major-leaguers wear. "It creates a sense of pride all the way up the ladder," said Macon coach Glenn Hubbard, reiterating the company line.

As the merchandise continued to sell at a rapid rate in the stadium's retail store, Hickory welcomed all the league's honorary Polecats, GreenJackets, Bombers, RedStixx, et al, on the field. The townspeople nearly filled the 5,200-seat stadium, dishing out six bucks for the cheap seats to an incredibly high twelve dollars for the best. The game was also televised by SportSouth, the Atlanta-based cable sports channel. Some of the players performed in front of cameras for the first time, and nearly all said they were glad to be there.

Carey Paige entered the season as a scared third-round draft pick and exited a major-league prospect. (Photo courtesy of Macon Braves)

"It's an honor. Everything they do for the players is great," said Dye, who played the first five innings in the N.L.'s 9-5 win. "I was real nervous when I first went out there," added Paige, who pitched the third inning. "Everything they have there is the best — the best field, lights, even a restaurant at the stadium. I've heard people say it won't be long before they have Double-A ball in Hickory."

Paige's progress in 1994 was not dissimilar to Hickory's in 1993. In fact, it would be difficult to find an all-star in the South Atlantic or any other minor league who had made greater strides in the first half of 1994 than Paige. A third-round draft pick out of Abilene, Texas, in 1992, the 20-year-old right-hander put together a pair of unimpressive seasons during his first two professional years. He was winless in 13 outings and three decisions in the Gulf Coast League the summer he signed, then registered a 4-2 mark and a 4.21 ERA at Danville in 1993.

"I felt like a mispick," Paige said. "I just felt like I wasn't what the Braves wanted."

His lack of confidence centered mainly on his lack of velocity. After consistently reaching 91 miles per hour on the radar gun during high school, Paige had trouble topping out at 86 at Danville. As his speed dropped, so did his faith and reliance in his abilities. Once he returned home after the 1993 season, he had begun to wonder if he hadn't made a major mistake somewhere along the way.

"I don't know how to explain it other than to say I was trying to do too much," Paige said. "You see all these pitchers every day and you try to be like them. I was trying to be someone else other than myself. I was trying to throw like this guy because he threw 95, or I was trying to throw like that guy because he had a good curveball. I just wasn't myself."

The discouraged Paige did not return to Texas and pout. Determined to at least improve his stamina, he undertook a detailed fitness routine outlined by the Braves that included weight lifting and running. His winter efforts left Paige physically stronger upon entering spring training, which helped him regain those previously lost miles per hour on his fastball.

His physical shape was only half the battle. In West Palm Beach, Paige met with roving pitching instructor Larry Rothschild, who wasted little time in making an accurate assessment of the young pitcher.

"He gave me a few questions," Paige said. "Before I had answered just a couple, he said, 'You have no confidence, I can already tell. You're a pitcher that pitches not to lose instead of one who pitches to win.' He was right. If I went out there in the first inning and some guy got a double, I wasn't thinking about that next batter. I was thinking about that guy on second base, worrying that he would score if the next guy got a hit. Instead, I needed to go out there and say, 'Screw you, you're not scoring.'

"Larry never did show me what to do. He just worked with my mind, the mental aspect of pitching. Now I go out there with a whole lot more confidence than I did last year."

His words were now being backed up with his performance on the field. Even though he pitched for a team that won only three of its first 26 outings and continued to struggle regularly at the plate, Paige owned a 6-6 record and an outstanding 2.23 ERA after 14 starts. More revealing was a handful of other numbers, including 87 strikeouts and 63 hits allowed in 76⅔ innings. Without his efforts, Macon's chances of being 28-41 at the break would be slim at best.

"I know my numbers could be even better, but that's why you don't worry about won-lost records," Paige said. "I mean, you'd like to have more wins than losses, but it's not a big deal. You go out and do your job, that's all you can ask for. The team will help you, but if they don't, you just try to do your best and go get them next time.

"Everything feels a lot better, and I'm real pleased with the way I've been throwing. I came to Macon wanting to have a better year than I had last year, and I think I'm doing that. If I keep pitching the way I have, I know that good things are going to come in the near future."

The Macon hitters had also picked up the pace after a dismal start. The primary offensive catalyst was Dye, who, like Paige, was overcoming events in his recent past to emerge as a top prospect. A pitcher during high school, Dye was beginning to post the kind of numbers the Braves had expected to see. Atlanta's only concern was that Dye and Paige and any other prospects would be able to overcome the losing and excel on their own. So far, that plan had been falling into place.

"I've talked with some of the top people and they tell me that this team has a lot of good prospects that are going to make it to the major leagues in a couple of years," Dye said. "We're sticking together real well. At first I thought we were going to break down. Everybody kind of dropped their heads after we lost all those games at the beginning. But we managed to remain positive and now our persistence is starting to pay off."

Making matters better was some offensive help for Dye. The late-May arrival of Charles "Gator" McBride had proven particularly beneficial. After beginning the year in extended spring training, McBride made his season debut May 29 with no nameplate on the back of his jersey, just the number 22. By the end of the Sunday afternoon contest versus Spartanburg, everyone at Luther Williams Field knew the versatile infielder/outfielder after he punched out a triple and a grand slam in Macon's 9-4 win over the Phillies.

Another late-May addition was also helping produce notches in the win column. Roger Ethridge, a southpaw twirler acquired from the Cincinnati organization as a throw-in in the Deion Sanders-for-Roberto Kelly deal at the major-league level, had more success than he experienced with the Charleston Wheelers. In four games with Macon, he was 2-1 with a respectable 3.38 ERA.

"It's real hard going from one team to another, especially in the middle of a season," Ethridge said in his heavy southern drawl. "You got a different manager, different rules. The main thing for me was not knowing anybody. The only person I knew was the roving pitching coach, Larry Rothschild, who used to be with the Reds. But everybody has treated me like I was one of the guys. That helped a lot."

As much as the strong play of Paige and Dye and the addition of McBride and Ethridge meant to Macon's improved performance, one man deserved as much credit as anyone. Leon Roberts had been as patient as a draft animal during April and May, all while building his players' confidence through a variety of techniques. He provided serious advice to some ("You gotta stay back. You're striding out, but everything is back here," Roberts told Dye in the batting cage.) and agitated others ("I've yet to see a player come out of Louisiana," he said to Danny Magee. "I mean, sure, you'll see a few guys come out and try, but they play like slow-pitch softball guys. I'm talking about overhand hardball, like we play in Texas. You don't see guys like that come out of Louisiana."). Everyone was beginning to agree that the recipe, much like the man, was nearly perfect.

"He never loses his composure," said Magee, Roberts' most frequent target. "He's always relaxed, always confident, and that's what we needed. At the beginning of the season, if he had started jumping on us, I think as a young team we would have reacted by just giving up. But he kept his composure and had confidence in us and we started playing better ball and progressing. Some managers would have gotten on our backs and made us work hard. All that would have done is tire us out and probably made us play even worse."

"Leon's player development first," Chuck LaMar said. "And that's why he's the perfect man for the job. The way we're set up and the way we're signing as many young players as possible, you need a man like Leon to guide very talented, very young, very inexperienced players. Because of that, once they wipe the slate clean at midseason, that Macon team will have a lot of fun in the second half."

Similar comments were echoed on the field in Hickory and during the early days of the second half. Macon had caused some teams to take note during the past month. No longer would disparaging comments be heard from smug opponents. If the trend continued, the Braves players could indeed wind up being the ones who laughed last and loudest.

"The rest of the league better watch out for these guys," said Asheville manager Tony Torchia, whose Tourists opened the second half in Macon. "They beat us for their first win, and even then you could see they had talent. Mark my words, they're going to gain some revenge against those who bad-mouthed them."

When the final out had been recorded on June 23, Macon had done in the first two nights of the second half what had taken three weeks to accomplish in the first half. The Braves had won two games. They also stood alone atop the Southern Division standings with a 2-0 record.

A Bullish Season

13

Something about baseball brings out the little boy in the game's participants. In spite of the stress, anguish and exhilaration experienced over the course of a minor-league season, most players wind up looking back on their days on the farm as some of their happiest moments life had to offer. Whether the memories consist of winning a pennant or drowning their sorrows, setting a teammate's shoelaces on fire in the clubhouse or swinging through a pitcher's best heater, the ups and downs that result from months of togetherness often make all the episodes worthwhile.

The Durham Bulls concluded the first half on an improving note. Frequently dreadful during the opening two months of the season, the team started to put together some timely hits and solid pitching performances in the days leading up to the midseason break. That momentum continued into the early days of the second half. The Bulls took all three games of the first series versus Winston-Salem and split four meetings at Kinston before opening an eight-game homestand that would carry through the long Fourth of July weekend. Matt West's words seemed to be sinking in. "We'll be a better team in the second half," the skipper repeated ad infinitum during the waning games of his club's last-place 28-40 record in the season's first half.

The winning ways begat a more relaxed clubhouse. Players did not walk as if their spikes were tip-toeing across egg shells, fearing another outburst from West as soon as something went awry. Though still businesslike in their work, the Bulls captured a more playful approach. The game was once again fun, and the results were being registered nightly on the scoreboard.

The looser mood momentarily shriveled up, however, on the final day of June. A seemingly innocent form of horseplay, an event that happens every afternoon on professional fields in every league, brought to an end the season of one Durham pitcher. Matt Byrd, a setup man with a 2-4 record and a 4.58 ERA, was shagging in the outfield during batting practice. As he reared back to toss another ball toward the midfield bucket, fellow hurler Tony Stoecklin ran behind Byrd in a playful attempt to take the stitched sphere out of his hand. Stoecklin wound up pulling Byrd's arm behind him, tearing most of the cartilage in Byrd's throwing shoulder. Byrd was scheduled to travel to Atlanta on July 6 to determine when to undergo the knife.

Byrd would not be traveling alone. Also headed south to be evaluated by Dr. Joe Chandler was Ken Giard. The 21-year-old right-hander had not pitched in three weeks because of discomfort in his throwing arm. His arm had been popping when he released the ball, creating severe pain. He had tried to put off medical attention by taking a cortisone shot 10 days earlier, but the pain resurfaced worse than before during a simple game of catch in the bullpen.

"I'm pretty much down about it," Giard said as he sat alone in the Durham dugout. His eyes, hidden in the back of his unshaven face, revealed his disappointment. "There's nothing I can really do other than just sit here and watch everybody every night. The best thing for me now is to get this fixed so I can come back with no problem at all."

This latest roadblock was not unfamiliar to Giard. Since signing with Atlanta as the Braves' 11th-round draft choice in 1991, the Rhode Island native's career had come across more detours than unobstructed paths. He began by failing to win a game while enduring minor physical ailments at Bradenton in 1991 and Idaho Falls in 1992. Giard then started to taste a little success in 1993, despite what his 1-7 record indicates. He led Macon in appearances, serving as a setup man and long reliever. But on the night he saved his first game, his career, as well as life as he knew it, came to an abrupt halt.

Giard had been living with an alcohol abuse problem since he was 15 years old. Similar to most problem drinkers, Giard's experience began innocently. He started by hanging out with his friends on weekends, when they would kill a six-pack or two of beer. Those outings led to a Thursday night, just to get a head start and extend the weekend. Giard's problem centered on the fact that he could not stop at one. Or two. Or three.

"As soon as I was done with high school and left to play ball, that was it," Giard said. The pitcher had little difficulty finding accompaniment after games in Bradenton and Idaho Falls. Once the players reached Macon in 1993, the team featured more major-league partiers than prospects. Often it seemed as if the players spent as much time at the Sports Spot, a favorite team hangout on Riverside Drive in Macon, as they did at Luther Williams Field.

The problem intensified for Giard during the winters. With no rigid schedule to follow, Giard continued to relive his high school days with his hometown friends. They visited watering holes more often, becoming a beer manufacturer's and recycling company's best client.

"I wasn't doing anything in the off-season to prepare myself to play the game," Giard said. "I would come to spring training overweight, out of shape and not ready to throw. During the season, I wasn't preparing myself for the games, doing the running that day or lifting weights. I just wasn't doing anything to prepare myself to do anything other than drink. I was coming to the field with hangovers, wasn't eating right, wasn't sleeping right.

"I was the type of person if I did good, I celebrated. If I did bad, I just wanted to forget about it and hang loose. As soon as the game was over, I'd take a shower, drink two beers, and I'd be off and running again. It helped a little to overcome the pressures of pro ball and all the little injuries I was experiencing. But more than anything, I always said that drinking helped pass the time. I always said I could quit, but I never really could."

The situation did have a fortunate side in that it did not take a catastrophic event to change Giard's ways. His lifestyle had done enough damage through lying to and cheating on the people closest to him. "I became the type of person who thought I was better than everybody else," Giard said. "I know I'm not. I know I'm supposed to respect people, and I wasn't doing that. I was blaming other people for things they didn't have a clue as to what I was talking about."

After registering a save in one of his better outings of the season, Giard again went out to celebrate with some 12-ounce curls. It was a night not unlike any other evening over the past few years. Only this evening, as he lay in bed in a drunken haze, burping beer and trying to avoid one of his ever-increasing blackouts, Giard somehow decided he had had enough.

The next morning, June 18, 1993, Giard arose and immediately headed over to the stadium to see manager Randy Ingle.

"I think it was the toughest thing I could ever say in my whole life," Giard said. "I had to tell him I had a drinking problem. But Randy made everything much easier. The day I told him, he sat there in his office and talked to me and told me he would do anything for me. I felt like my whole life was going down the drain and he was there doing everything he could."

Giard asked Ingle to help. Ingle responded by contacting the Braves front office. Two days later, Giard was admitted to Anchor Hospital in Atlanta, where he underwent the facility's 30-day program.

"My first couple of days in the hospital, when I started hearing all the crazy stories, I said, 'I'm not one of these people,'" Giard said. "I talked to a doctor and he said, 'Try to identify with these people, don't try to compare yourself with them.' I started listening to them and started getting involved with their conversations and pretty soon it worked out great."

His first day or so in the program was made tougher because he felt weak compared to his teammates. That feeling soon changed when most of the Macon players showed their support by calling or sending cards. Instead of being perceived as a loser, he was deemed heroic. That support made the entire process much easier when in early August, the newest member of Alcoholics Anonymous rejoined the Braves for the season's final month.

"I was lucky, 'cause I really didn't hit bottom like other people have," Giard said. "Before this arm injury, I felt incredible, and I still do. I run every day. Before, I never ran, and if I did, I'd cut myself short or end up vomiting. I'd pitch an inning and I was done. I was so tired all the time. I feel like a new person now. I never thought a substance like that could do something as bad as what alcohol did to me. I'm just so glad I'm not part of that any more. Right now I feel like I'll never ever go back to it."

Instead of hitting the college taverns the surrounding area offered, Giard returned home to his apartment with roommates Byrd, Jamie Arnold and Darrell May. Their postgame excitement consisted of playing cards, ordering a couple pizzas or watching *SportsCenter* on ESPN. Giard admitted that he was not ready to go out on the town just yet. There was no reason to put himself in a situation that could only unravel a year's worth of work.

"If I don't make that decision to go into recovery, I'm not too sure I'd still be playing today," Giard said. "It was a bad situation, and I think everything is going to be better for me in the long run. I don't know what's wrong with my arm, but I know it can't be harder to overcome than everything I've gone through since last June. That's all I care about right now, playing baseball and taking care of myself."

Giard and Byrd were not the only losses the Durham pitching staff suffered during the last week of June. On Monday the 27th, the Bulls lost the hurler who had emerged as the staff ace. Matt Murray overcame his early-season disappointment to regain the form he expected to display. In his last six outings, the right-hander dropped his earned run average nearly two full runs, to 3.97, and improved his record to 6-7. Those performances were rewarded with a promotion to Greenville.

Several reasons bred Murray's improvement. After watching his fastball become high and flat in the strike zone, the right-hander worked on a two-seam heater with pitching coach Bill Slack. The quality two-seamer added another moving pitch to his repertoire which gave hitters something else to think about.

Slack also worked with Murray on his mental approach. By constantly drilling the phrase, "The ink is dry from the last pitch," Slack convinced Murray to quit worrying about what had happened with the previous batter and to concentrate on the task at hand.

"It was weird. It really wasn't my stuff so much, it was just my whole attitude," Murray said. "You hate to say it, but I guess being pissed off about starting in Durham affected me. I was getting down on myself. I had a talk with Bill Slack and Matt West. They both told me, 'Hey, you're worrying too much about the results. You're not thinking about the progress you're making as far as the things you were working on in spring training.' I just assumed I'd go there and dominate, but I wasn't even close."

Murray believed the turning point to his season came after his poorest outing, against Wilmington on April 29. That's when his priest told Murray afterwards how proud he was of the young pitcher's effort. "It just totally woke me up," said Murray, who came close several times in late April to hanging up the glove and spikes for good. "And even the next start I didn't pitch all that well, but I didn't let it affect me.

"It was hard to come to the park in April. I guess you just need a wake-up call every once in a while that makes you realize that there are a million people who would love to be doing what you're doing. And the fact that I've worked so hard to come back from my surgery, it would really be a shame if I didn't give it all I had. I swore I'd never quit."

His overhauled attitude in place, Murray went out and put together an outstanding June. He opened the month with a 5-3 win at Lynchburg before defeating the Red Sox again six days later, 4-1. The 9-1 victory at Salem followed on June 12, succeeded by a 9-5 loss to Wilmington on June 18, his only weak outing of the month. On June 23, he tossed his best game of the year, a 2-1 decision over Winston-Salem, which set the stage for Sunday afternoon, June 26, a day before he was to take the mound again.

Murray entered the visiting clubhouse of Kinston's Grainger Stadium, his light blue workout shirt turned almost black from the sweat in the suffocating heat and humidity of eastern North Carolina. As he walked by the manager's cubby-hole, West yelled to the right-hander.

"Oh, by the way, I need to talk to you."

"What is it?" Murray asked as he stood dripping in the doorway.

"You're going to Greenville tomorrow, but I still need you to do the game chart for me tonight."

Murray isn't sure what he did next. "I was definitely pumped," Murray said. "It was almost like a sigh of relief. Finally I'm going to get a shot at Double-A. Obviously I didn't deserve it early on, but when I finally started pitching well, I thought I deserved it. The Braves said from the beginning that as soon as I earned it, I'd move up. Sure enough, they did it. Sometimes organizations don't keep their word, but the Braves did."

Despite the loss of three pitchers, the Bulls continued their winning ways. They opened the long homestand by splitting their first two games with Salem before Mike D'Andrea put together one of the best performances and only the second shutout of the year for Durham. The Bulls then claimed their fourth victory in five outings by upending Salem, 9-3, on July 1. Mike Warner continued to prove that a promotion to Greenville was in his future by leading off the first, third and fifth innings with hits, scoring every time. Warner's bat caused the scouts sitting in The Dap's reserved blue seats to take note.

"That boy has a chance to play for a couple other teams," said one scout. "He's hitting the ball all over the place."

"Yeah, but I'll leave and he won't get a hit for the rest of the season. Last year, I came here and he got eight straight hits. Then he didn't do a thing from there."

"You know, I went back and looked at my notes and he didn't show me shit," said a third. "But he's looking a hell of a lot better than what he showed last year."

Hector Roa, a 23-year-old shortstop who joined the Bulls June 24 while recovering from surgery on a broken left thumb, joined Warner in providing his fair share of offense. He singled up the middle in the third to score Warner, then crushed a two-out, 1-1 pitch for a home run in the seventh to give the Bulls a comfortable 6-2 lead. But the team was not especially pleased by the end result.

There was little doubt that Roa got all of Chris Peters' offering. The Dominican could feel the baseball jump off his bat, and he stood at home plate and admired the white projectile disappear deep into the dark Durham sky. He ignored the command to get moving from Salem catcher Jason Kendall as well as the icy glares from Peters. Roa then added salt to the wound by practically walking to first base before taking a slow jog around the rest of the diamond.

Many of the players in the Durham dugout became as outraged as Peters and Kendall. That it was Roa putting on such a show only made matters worse. A talented ballplayer who was once considered among Atlanta's top 20 prospects, Roa's self-centered attitude and constant trouble-making had made him as popular as the Internal Revenue Service. And the fact that the Braves did little to reprimand the shortstop for his misdeeds simply added fuel to his disgruntled teammates' fire.

When the show finally ended and Roa arrived in the dugout, he was greeted by Brad Rippelmeyer, who collared and threatened the shortstop about putting the rest of the team at risk. Embarrassing an opponent is not tolerated at any level of baseball. Revenge is almost always imminent. Rippelmeyer's feelings intensified an inning later when Marty Malloy felt Peters' wrath with a fastball that ricochetted off his batting helmet. Malloy, the most intense Bull, removed his helmet, slammed it to the ground, and stared menacingly at Roa in the dugout.

Such disruptive behavior had become commonplace for Roa. He had frustrated nearly everyone since signing with the Braves as a free agent out of the Dominican Republic in 1989. Whether it was failing to run out ground balls, piling up hundreds of dollars in unpaid long-distance phone bills and clubhouse dues, or suffering from an unknown illness or ailment on nights he simply did not want to play, Roa was little more than an organizational cancer. On those rare evenings when he took the field and played hard, his skills shined. His arm was strong in the hole, his bat powerful for a middle infielder. The problem was, those nights had become fewer and fewer in recent years.

Defenders of Roa, what few exist, counter his teammates' beliefs by saying the shortstop is a product of the minors. He, like other Latin Americans, was plucked by a major-league organization from a predominantly poor environment at a young age for pocket change and a chance for riches in another world. Most have never left their native country, not to mention traveled to the United States. Throw in the fact that practically none of the players speaks English, and it is little wonder only a small percentage of the foreign players signed ever reach the major leagues.

Most Latin players in the low minors rarely interact with their American teammates. They hang out together at one end of the dugout or one corner of the clubhouse, relying on the one who speaks the best broken English to communicate with the coaching staff. It is not unusual to see all Latins living in the same apartment, even if there are seven or eight on the team. Most of them do so to save as much of their paychecks as possible, since the amounts are typically more money than anyone in their families has seen at one time.

The Braves try to soften the culture shock by having a Spanish-speaking coach with their low minor-league clubs. But that was not the case in 1990, when Roa was promoted from Bradenton to Pulaski. Roa was for a while the only person on the team who spoke Spanish, causing him to feel like an outcast. When the Braves would make a fast-food stop while on the road, he always ordered last by pointing to whatever the player in front of him purchased, regardless of whether he liked it. One day his teammates made Roa order first at a Hardee's.

"Big Delusion," Roa, meaning a Big Deluxe, told the cashier. His teammates nearly fell on the restaurant floor in laughter. Roa tried to smile as he looked around, wondering what had happened to create the laugh riot.

Roa had since learned to communicate in English when convenient. Other Latins make no effort to master the language. They instead learn the basics, such as "bus leaves at ten o'clock", "early BP" and "no game tomorrow."

"There are a lot of Dominican people that started with me and to this day they speak no English," said Atlanta catcher Javy Lopez. "My advice to the Puerto Ricans, Dominicans, the first thing you have to do here is learn the language. If you can do that, then you can learn from and deal with anybody. There are a lot of coaches that can help you. If you don't speak to them, they're not going to help you at all. English is not easy. But if you take the time and the trouble to learn it, it can do nothing but help you."

Lopez knows of what he speaks. He was never considered a prospect until he became fluent in English in 1990 and 1991. Prior to becoming bilingual, he had trouble calling games. He could not converse with the pitchers or the managers, which left him as little more than a human pitch-back net behind the plate.

Asked if English was Roa's problem, Lopez smiled and shook his head. "Hector is the type of guy who doesn't try to learn," Lopez said. "It doesn't matter if he spoke English or not. You never know what Hector's going to do."

Few people would disagree with Lopez. Taking aspirin for the headaches Roa had caused over the years would be the equivalent of dousing a forest fire with cups of water. The most serious event involving the shortstop took place in West Palm Beach at the end of spring training in 1993. Roa allegedly battered a woman who had sex with another player but refused to do the same with him. The case was settled out of court, with part of Roa's paycheck sent to the woman's attorney every two weeks.

At other times, Roa has gone beyond the call of duty to be accommodating. When Michael Jordan gave Roa an autographed bat in late April, Roa turned around and presented it to one of Greenville's clubhouse employees. He also thanked a young fan for congratulating him on a fine defensive play by autographing a baseball for the youngster during the course of a game.

But on the evening of July 1, Roa's diabolic side created a furor among the Bulls. Coach Rick Albert lectured Roa after the game. His most ardent point focused on how fortunate everything turned out. Malloy was not injured, nor were any other players because of retaliatory efforts.

The Bulls also wound up with sweet revenge after Malloy was plunked. Malloy stole second and remained there as Rippelmeyer coaxed a two-out walk from Peters. Tom Waldrop stepped in the left batter's box, watched two pitches that were called balls, then lined the third toss over the right-field wall to help seal the 9-3 victory.

"It was a 2-0 count," Waldrop said. "If you've noticed in this league, 2-0, 3-1 counts, they're going to challenge lefty on lefty. It's kind of a mind game."

The first three months of the season had turned into one long mind bender for Waldrop. A slow April concluded with the hottest week any Brave minor-leaguer put together in 1994. Mid-May brought more troubles at the plate, which led to Waldrop's platooning through most of June. By July 1, his batting average was a mere .213. His home run that evening was his eighth of the year, but his first in three weeks.

"This year's been a roller coaster ride," Waldrop said. "It hasn't gone the way I wanted it to go. One of these years I'm going to get off to a good start instead of a bad one."

Waldrop was asked if he, as a player signed as an undrafted free agent, ever worried that next year might not come, especially considering another batch of players had been drafted and the Braves had little money invested in the outfielder's career.

"Yeah, it goes through everybody's mind when they're in that situation," Waldrop said. "Matt West talked to me a couple times and told me not to press, not to worry about that. My job's not at stake. They know what I can do, so just relax, go up there, and hit the ball.

"I think some of my problems have come from not starting every day. It's something everybody has a hard time doing. I've been sitting on the bench for seven innings, coming up to pinch-hit, and that's something I wasn't used to. We talked about that, and I tried to change my mentality a little bit. Hopefully now I'm going to get in there because I'm hitting the ball again."

Waldrop's heroics coincidentally came in front of his dad, who was in Durham for Tom's hot streak in late April and had not returned since. Joining Bud Waldrop for this trip was Tom's mother, Sally, and girlfriend, Natalie, all of whom led The Dap in cheers when the outfielder went deep in the eighth inning.

"I used to get nervous when they came to games in college, but they've all seen me hit," Waldrop said of his cheering section. "They know I can hit the ball. It's not like if I don't do good in front of them, they're going to think I'm not a good player. They more or less know what I can do, so there's no pressure."

Bud, Sally and Natalie were at The Dap long before game time the following afternoon. They had joined Tom for lunch earlier in the day when the party used the twenty-five dollar certificate Waldrop won in late April by hitting the snorting bull on a home run over the right-field wall. "We needed it," Bud said. "Our bill for lunch was $62.00."

Waldrop telephones his parents every evening following the game after talking with his 92-year-old grandmother nearly every afternoon. Though baseball is often the topic, it is only when Tom brings up the subject. "We don't talk much about baseball when things aren't going well for him," Sally said. "We don't ask; we just let him tell us. But no matter what he does, we're so proud of him. I never thought he'd get the opportunity to play or get this far."

Baseball was most assuredly the subject for the next two days. Energized by the steak dinner, Waldrop went 2-for-4 with another home run in as many nights to help the Bulls overcome a six-run deficit and defeat Frederick, 8-7. He continued to excel in front of his family on Sunday evening, hitting another three-run homer in Durham's 13-12 win over the Keys. With three roundtrippers in as many nights, no one would have been surprised if Waldrop started searching for housing in the Durham area for his apparent good-luck charms.

"It's a confidence-builder," Waldrop said. "I just think that when I did get in my groove earlier, people started to pitch me differently and I didn't handle it real good. I didn't make the necessary adjustments to keep in the groove. Now I'm making the adjustment to every pitch.

"I've seen the other side, too. It's really tough when you're sitting on the bench and you're in the middle of an oh-for-fifteen. That's when depression comes in. When you get out there after not playing, you don't know how many at bats you're going to have this week. You want every one to count. You have to concentrate and not waste any, but you also have to relax.

"Now my main thing is, I want to finish strong and keep my confidence up to where it is now and not get down on myself if I do have a couple bad nights. I attribute this little streak here to knowing the pitcher I'm facing. It kind of gets my mentality set, my approach to when I go to the plate about what I want to do."

Waldrop's bat again cooled once his family returned to the Midwest. The Bulls, meanwhile, continued to play at a pace as warm as the weather. Durham won 12 of its first 17 July games before the three-day Carolina League All-Star break. Mike Warner, Jamie Arnold, Darrell May, Damon Hollins and Robert Smith represented the Bulls in Wilmington, Delaware, before returning to The Dap and helping the club finish the month with a 15-10 record.

Durham continued to surprise the rest of the league by maintaining a five-game stranglehold on first place in the Southern Division on August 1. After a disappointing first-half showing, things appeared to have turned around. Maybe, just maybe, The Dap would go out a winner in its second final season.

Hurricane Bruce

14

The dark, ominous clouds floated and hung over Greenville Municipal Stadium on June 28 like jellyfish in the ocean. Thunderstorms had become frequent visitors in recent nights, soaking the unsheltered fans in each of the G-Braves' previous two home games with Huntsville. And though about 75 patrons sat through the elements on the Tuesday night while listening to the public address announcer hawk the ponchos and umbrellas available for purchase at the souvenir stand, the lightning, rain and gloominess offered little hope for baseball.

The mood was much different in the press box. Members of the front office stared intently at the weather radar on the television screen, cheering as the pattern turned from green to yellow to red, indicating a more violent storm that would surely wash away any chance of playing the game. For most full-time minor-league employees, a rainout in the middle of a long homestand conjures up childhood memories of wishing for snow and an unexpected holiday from school.

Ten minutes prior to game time, general manager Steve DeSalvo pulled the plug. The game was off and would be made up in Huntsville in mid-July. High-fives were exchanged in between the whoops and hollers that filled the press box. "I can get home by nine tonight," said Matt Garvey, still wet from having to help drag the tarp onto the diamond a half-hour earlier. The rainout meant that the public relations director's work day would be 12 hours in length instead of the expected 15.

Similar emotions emitted from the Greenville clubhouse. Players pulled off their uniforms, jumped into their clothes, and within minutes of the cancellation were screeching out of the rain-soaked parking lot in their cars in search of what the night might offer.

Storms, many of them violent, continued to pelt the upstate area for the remainder of the night. Yet their intensity and ferocity could not come close to equalling what Hurricane Bruce possessed on the previous Saturday evening. The Greenville manager put forth an effort that left many of the 8,000 in attendance shaking their heads in amazement.

The storm had gained strength throughout the season's first half. Benedict believed that his team had been on the short end of several controversial calls from the two-man umpiring crew of Andy Fletcher and Brian King. When the skipper politely questioned a few of the calls at a later date, he felt that the two umps, especially Fletcher, refused to even concede the plays had been close. The number of such plays seemed to increase every time Fletcher and King worked a G-Braves game, a fact that caused Benedict to grow increasingly upset.

Those feelings did nothing but intensify in the series opener with the Stars. Fletcher was calling balls and strikes, and Benedict started riding the home-plate umpire soon after the contest commenced. After a couple of innings that produced an especially wide strike zone for Greenville's hitters, the pressure finally became too intense and the storm erupted.

Tim Gillis was at the plate and took the first pitch, a chest-high slider that Fletcher called a strike. Gillis looked back at Fletcher but said nothing. Benedict, meanwhile, was seething. Fletcher glared twice toward the dugout, practically begging the manager to become more vocal. Those glances were all it took for the skipper to head toward home plate.

"You do it and you're gone," yelled Fletcher.

Benedict took four steps toward home plate, did an about-face, grabbed a towel and resumed his march. He wasted little time in calling Fletcher the magic word, to which the umpire responded by ejecting the manager from the game. Undaunted, Benedict turned around and wiped off home plate with the towel before proving that a mime career could be in the offing. With all the theatrics of a Broadway play, Benedict measured with his hands the height and width of the strike zone. He completed the act by going face-to-face with Fletcher before King stepped in to try to bring the impromptu meeting to a halt.

King's efforts proved futile. Every time the umpire stepped between the two combatants, Benedict jumped around the human obstacle. Before long, Benedict's dialogue consisted of f-bombs and you and little else.

"Bruce, you've said that so many times, I'm beginning to believe that's what you really want to do," King said, which only agitated Benedict further. When the storm finally cleared the field, 10 minutes had elapsed. Benedict received a standing ovation from the home crowd as he walked down the right-field line toward the Greenville clubhouse. He also soon became the recipient of a three-day suspension, handed down by Southern League president Jimmy Bragan.

Every player has a handful of stories about run-ins with umpires. Most wear their disagreements like badges of honor. And while no detailed research has been conducted to support the claim, most of the game's participants feel the battles are becoming more frequent and that the situation is on the verge of getting out of hand.

"I admit I don't like most umpires," said Mike Mordecai. "They're too interested in determining the wins and losses and that's not their job. You shouldn't even notice them, like in a boxing match, where the best referees aren't even seen. It's not like that in baseball anymore. An umpire thinks you're showing them up any time you question a call. They slow down the game by trying to control everything, and they'll run you in a heartbeat. That combative attitude they have is coming from somewhere, because practically every umpire in every league is like that."

Greenville Braves manager Bruce Benedict in a happier moment. (Photo courtesy of Greenville Braves)

Matt Murray had been ejected once in his career. It came during his final start of the 1993 season. The umpire missed several calls in the first inning, refusing to give the right-hander either side of the plate. After two men had walked, Murray finally grooved a pitch down the middle. The batter crushed the ball into the right-center field gap, creating a merry-go-round on the basepaths. As he ran past the plate to back up the catcher, Murray yelled, "Those are yours." Before the play concluded, the umpire raised his fist in the air and histrionically ejected the pitcher.

"For all he knew I could have been yelling at my catcher, which I wasn't," Murray said. "It was ridiculous. The guy was just seeing how far he could push it. I gave him an earful before I left, but the situation should have never happened."

Despite the complaints, most umpires put forth an honest effort, if for no other reason than to advance their careers. They also experience the pressures of the game, a role that supervisor and former major-league umpire Jerry Neudecker says, "It's the only job in the world where you're expected to be perfect your first day and improve from there." And until a computerized system can be developed that will remove the human element from split-second decisions, the battles that date to the beginning of the game will continue to occur.

His at bat may have triggered Benedict's explosion, but Gillis had few complaints about the umpiring or any other aspect of baseball during the latter half of June. He began the season with one of his notorious slow starts and continued to struggle through most of the team's second-place, 36-32 first half. Much like fine wine, Gillis' bat merely needed time to ferment before producing the desired result. The veteran hit safely in 13 of 15 outings in late June, with his .380 clip upping his batting average to .273. Power accompanied his improved percentage, with Gillis posting three of his five homers and 10 of his team-high 33 RBIs during the stretch.

Gillis' rebound coincided with a painful bone bruise at the base of his right hand. The ailment kept him from holding the bat at the knob, and forced him to choke up a couple of inches. The adjustment initially felt awkward, but his bat was a little quicker since the grip took much of the loop out of his swing. He had become a more productive member of the offense and enabled the G-Braves to finish the first half on a strong note.

"I pressed hard to get off to a good start, then I didn't and it took a while to get out of a bad groove," Gillis said a week after Benedict's outburst, while sitting in the visiting dugout of Carolina's Five County Stadium. "I've been feeling pretty good for the past month. Now I have a chance if I keep doing what I'm doing to get back around .300."

What he had done earned Gillis the Southern League's batter-of-the-week honors. To some, the award came with an asterisk. Bragan altruistically tried to recognize every team during the season. That meant the weekly awards honoring a top hitter and pitcher did not necessarily go to the appropriate party. Had the deserving player recently received the recognition or if other players from his team won the award in the preceding weeks, chances are the award would go to someone else on another team. Gillis nonetheless welcomed the acknowledgment.

"It means something to me," Gillis said. "I also got it two years ago in this league. I think it's a pretty big honor. It's not something you're shooting for, but if you get it, it at least means you had a good week."

The recognition was well-deserved for more subtle reasons. In addition to his hitting contributions, Gillis' versatility and unselfishness in the field had made the G-Braves a stronger club. He moved across the diamond to first base during the 1993 season, even though his ability at the hot corner had been rated best in the Atlanta farm system just two years earlier. He continued to learn and excel at the new position during the early stages of 1994 before a move was needed to insert the bat of Kevin Grijak into the lineup. Since Grijak was a liability anywhere on the field other than first, and with third baseman

Ed Giovanola having been promoted to Richmond, Gillis shook off the rust and shifted back to third without so much as a peep.

"I don't think the defensive move had anything to do with my struggles at the plate," Gillis said. "To me it's two totally different games, and you need to be able to separate it as a player. Because sometimes if you're not going good at the plate, you wind up taking it out to the field and it kills you. You have to separate the two and do both jobs."

Thunder began to build in the distance as Gillis reflected on the first three months of the 1994 season. The infielder was asked if he ever heard rumors or worried about the status of his career during stretches like the one he endured in April and May.

"Sure. You think that it could all come to an end at any time," Gillis said. "I'm 26 years old in Double A. You think, 'Man, if I don't start doing something, they're going to put a younger guy up here.' I try not to think about that, just like I try to put making it to Triple A and the majors out of my mind. I still envision myself playing for the Braves. I'd love to play in Atlanta. Until that happens, it's like the old cliche, you got to take it one day at a time and just see what happens. That's the thing about this game. It's today. It's not tomorrow and it's not yesterday. It's all today."

Gillis' words brought to mind what former G-Braves pitcher Lee Upshaw used to preach. Upshaw quoted his father, Cecil, a former reliever for Atlanta in the late 1960s and early 1970s, when he said, "In baseball, you can't worry about anything but today. If you have one foot in the past and one foot in the future, you're just pissing on today." Few words held more truth for any minor-leaguer.

On this today, the G-Braves dropped another decision to the Mudcats in Carolina, and within minutes of the defeat, the Greenville bus was headed west along Interstate 40, beginning a six-hour journey toward Knoxville. Taking the mound the next evening would be Terrell Wade. Once again the left-hander had to pitch following an all-night ride in bus seats built for Lilliputians. Such trips were the bane of playing in the Southern League, the circuit noted as having the minors' worst bus rides.

No one would admit to enjoying bus rides, even if they do have their positive points. The trips bring many teams closer together. The players engross themselves in card games and tell stories about previous experiences with baseball, girls and carousing. Greenville's bus is equipped with a video cassette recorder, and prior to every trip a sheet is passed around to vote on the movie to be shown.

There are rules, passed down by the Atlanta front office, that forbid the consumption of alcohol and tobacco products on bus trips, no stereos unless equipped with head phones, and no sleeping in the luggage racks. The coaching staff sits in the seats closest to the front, with the remaining players staking out territories that typically remain intact all season. The lone exception comes in allowing the next game's starting pitcher to stretch out on the back seat, which sits three or four instead of two. By the time the destination is reached, newspapers are strewn everywhere in between the arms and legs that loom from all directions.

Regardless of the lodging accommodations, Wade continued to excel. In Knoxville on July 3, he overcame the discomforts of minor-league travel to shut down the Smokies before reliever Brad Clontz suffered the loss in the 2-1 final. Wade led the team with eight wins and ranked second in the league with 88 whiffs. Those numbers helped him earn a spot on the National League team in the Double-A All-Star Game in Binghamton, New York, on July 11. Clontz also received the recognition, as did Greenville second baseman Tony Graffanino.

"I got good command of my fastball, and I need to get my curveball over a little more," Wade said while peering out from under the bill of his cap, which was pulled down so far it nearly touched his nose. "I'm just trying to stayed focused. Lately I might mess up and walk the bases loaded and have to come out of the game. I can't afford to be doing that, letting the reliever clean up my mess. Our bullpen is really doing a good job, but I got to be more consistent with the strike zone."

Appearing relaxed on the bullpen bench, Wade suddenly displayed his feline reflexes by pouncing on an unsuspecting teammate and applying a front-face headlock. After coaxing the desired self-incriminating phrase from his victim, Wade got up, put his cap back on, and laughed before falling back on the bench as if nothing had happened.

There was no denying the pitcher has fun at work. Asked what he would be doing if he had never been discovered in the South Carolina tryout camp, Wade snickered and shrugged his shoulders.

"I'm 21 now. I guess I'd probably be in my last year of college," Wade said. "I was going to college to play basketball at Knoxville Junior College. I think it was a two-year college, and then I would have transferred to another school. If not that, then I'd be working with my brother or something like that."

How about earning a few bucks while hustling pool?

"Yeah, that too," Wade said with a grin and a wink. "But I can still do that."

Hard-Nosed Baseball

15

"Can you believe we're 10 games over .500?" Grady Little muttered while leaning against the back of the batting cage one mid-July evening.

The Richmond skipper was not the only one with raised eyebrows, for the R-Braves had been the International League's biggest surprise during the first three months of the season. The team was never out of first place by more than 3½ games during April and May, and held the top spot in the I.L. West for 16 of 17 days in June. The first two weeks of July had brought more success, including three straight wins to open the month and an overall record of 52-39 entering the all-star break.

"This is a hard-nosed bunch of guys who aren't going to quit on you," Little said, turning up the volume. "Our pitchers have been keeping us in the games, and the hitters are scratching out runs. We don't have a lot of long-ball hitters, which has led to a bad time or two. But everything considered, we're doing well."

The midyear break can be a difficult period for players at all minor-league levels, especially those in Triple-A. The three days off give a player time to consider and evaluate his progress. Does the organization still have plans for me? Has my stock risen or fallen in the scouts' eyes? Is my future in baseball, or does the working world become reality in two months? Players that become anxious begin to press, which not only hurts their performances, it also makes the manager's job more difficult. Managing 23 players into a progressive unit is tough enough, but to do so when some of those are on the verge of schizophrenia can border on the impossible.

"Staying focused is the toughest part during this time of year," Little said. "Guys start worrying about where they're playing and how they're playing. They're looking at who's ahead of them in the organization and worrying if they're ever going to get a chance in Atlanta. They're worrying about where they'll be playing next year. They hear about the draft and start thinking about where they stand in the organization.

"Instead of that, they ought to stay focused and do the things that are going to make them better players. Now that the draft is over, the scouts are all over the place looking at these guys. If they're playing well, who knows? Maybe they'll get a shot with another club. Sometimes it's hard to stay focused with all that's going on in the game, but it's definitely in their best interests to do so."

Three of the primary reasons the R-Braves had enjoyed their unexpected success could be attributed to the team's three representatives in the Triple-A All-Star Game. Left-hander Brad Woodall tossed two perfect innings and wound up being credited with the victory after entering the contest with a 12-4 record, best in the minor-leagues. Reliever Terry Clark, who led the league with 21 saves, tossed one scoreless frame in the all-star game. And first baseman Luis Lopez was named the most valuable player among the International League honorees by recording three hits in four trips to the plate with two runs scored and a pair of RBIs.

The season put together by Woodall had been the most surprising of the three all-stars. Bypassed out of the University of North Carolina, Woodall thought his baseball days were over until he worked out for Braves scout Roy Clark a few days after the 1991 draft. Until that fortuitous tryout, Woodall was hoping to put his economics degree to use with a local bank.

"I thought my baseball career was over until Roy offered me a contract," Woodall said. "I didn't know anything about pro ball. I went out to Idaho Falls just to play for the summer, just to see what it was like and how far it took me. I considered not signing because I didn't want to have my career as a real person delayed. My mom was against it, but my dad told me that in 10 years I might want to have the opportunity back. But I still didn't think my career was going to go any further than that."

Neither did the Braves until Woodall showed some promise by leading the Pioneer League with 11 saves and gaining a spot on the circuit's postseason all-star team. That showing earned him a brief trip to Durham at schedule's end before splitting the 1992 campaign as a reliever at Durham and Greenville. An elbow problem set him back at the beginning of the following season, the same year Woodall wound up becoming a starter, pitching at Durham, Greenville and Richmond, and winning 10 games against eight defeats.

His resiliency was admirable in his first three years, but no one thought Woodall would emerge as a bona fide prospect in 1994. Employing a change-up that led one scout to say, "The hitters know it's coming, but they still can't hit it," the southpaw succeeded with impeccable control and a variety of off-speed pitches peppered with a decent fastball. The numbers spoke volumes, yet some opponents still could not believe it.

"A guy like me who doesn't throw hard, I know I'm not going to be very impressive to look at," Woodall said. "I got to really put up good numbers and get guys out consistently to open people's eyes.

"The key to my success is, it's been a total learning process over the past three years that's now paying off. It's also a matter of confidence. I went to winter ball this past off-season and faced some big-league hitters. I found out I could actually get them out after looking up to those guys so much. They're hitters, real people, just like anybody else. They may be good, but they're not so good that I can't get them out."

Despite Woodall's continued success in mid-July, the R-Braves fell into their first extended tailspin since mid-May. Richmond returned from the break by dropping a 6-2 decision to Norfolk at The Diamond before Mike Birkbeck suffered his first loss since May 11 in a 5-0 Tides' win at Harbor Park. Norfolk looked to extend its victory string to three over the R-Braves a night later, July 19, and appeared to be on its way with a 2-1 lead in the top of the eighth.

A one-run deficit was not considered a major hurdle, not for a team like Richmond, which refused to accept defeat without battling until all 27 outs had been exhausted. And that deficit was soon erased with two outs in the eighth when Mike Mordecai tied the game at 2-2 with a solo homer, his 12th roundtripper of the year. Lopez followed by coaxing a walk from pitcher Dave Telgheder and was replaced at first base by pinch-runner Troy Hughes.

With a runner on first and two outs, the scoring threat was still considered mild. That threat was minimized even further when the next batter bounced a harmless ground ball to the third baseman. Regardless of the low odds, Hughes took off toward second to break up the force out. But instead of a play at the keystone sack, Hughes made the turn and accelerated toward third after Norfolk third sacker Butch Huskey allowed the ball to trickle through his legs. The ball rested in shallow left field, and Hughes continued to motor around the bases, now headed toward home. Tides left fielder Rick Parker finally retrieved the ball and hurled a near-perfect strike to the plate, where catcher Joe Kmak made the grab and waited for Hughes to arrive.

Hard-nosed baseball was a trait of this Richmond team, and Hughes was not about to ruin the reputation. Running as if a championship were on the line, Hughes cleanly lowered his shoulder and created a collision in his attempt to jar the ball loose from Kmak's mitt. The impact was more a brush than a high-impact crash. Kmak maintained possession of the ball after making the tag. Hughes was out, the Richmond rally dead.

"I got up and was going to pat him on the butt and say 'Good play'," said Hughes, referring to Kmak. "All the sudden, he's shouting at me, trying to push his glove in my face."

A shoving match quickly erupted. When home plate umpire Jim Wheeler separated the two combatants, Telgheder pushed Hughes from behind and grabbed the runner's head. The dugouts emptied and tensions elevated, but order was restored before any further altercations broke out. The entire ordeal turned out to be little more than a junior-high homecoming dance.

Three more scoreless innings followed until Brian Kowitz's single to center scored Bobby Moore in the top of the 12th and provided the R-Braves with a 3-2 win. Richmond's elation was short-lived, however, and not just because the team dropped its next four contests, including a three-game sweep to Rochester at The Diamond.

Word came from International League president Randy Mobley that 15 of Richmond's 23 players were suspended two games and fined $300 each because of the fracas with Norfolk. Citing the rule adopted prior the 1994 season in an effort to reduce the number of bench-clearing brawls in the minors that fines and suspends any player leaving his position during a rhubarb, Mobley announced that two Richmond players and one pitcher would be suspended at a time. Norfolk received the same treatment, with all but three of the Tides' players being penalized.

Stunned upon learning their fate, the R-Brave players soon voiced their displeasure over a couple of Mobley's decisions. The greatest complaint involved the lack of action taken against Kmak and Telgheder. The umpire reports, which named Richmond outfielder Beau Allred as an offender even though he was in Atlanta receiving medical attention, listed Hughes, not the taunting Kmak, as the instigator. Mobley backed up the report by stating the catcher had not left his position.

"I believe that the rule as it has been stated is a joke," Mordecai said. "Baseball is baseball and you're going to have some guys get hot under the collar and things happen. You don't even think about the consequences.

"I can understand what they're trying to do. But it was the heat of the battle. It was a tight ballgame. That was the go-ahead run for us. Two sides get fired up playing ball, and there's a big play at the plate. The guys are cheering and out of the dugout and the next thing you know, they're taking $300 out of your pocket. The play was strictly emotional, and the rule is trying to take some emotion out of the game."

Mobley admitted that taking $300 was harsh, especially considering the end result. At the same time, said the president, rules are rules. And this new rule obviously was having some effect. Bench-clearing brawls occurred in the International League seven times in 1993 prior to July 1. Since the rule had been implemented over the winter to keep hockey matches from breaking out on minor-league diamonds, the Norfolk-Richmond affair had been the first of 1994.

The president's sympathy notwithstanding, the reality of paying the fines started to hit home once the anger subsided. Richmond's roster consisted of few bonus babies or higher-salaried veterans. The players' paychecks provided little more than a meager existence, and a $300 reduction from one check could prove devastating. Rent payments had to be met, various bills had to be paid. The impact was felt even harder by Chris Seelbach and Brad Clontz, the recently promoted players who were still receiving the Double-A salary of $1,300 a month.

Money, predictably, became the topic of conversation before, during and after games for the next several days until all the talk produced a brainstorm from the Richmond players. Why not raise the money through some community-related events? The more the subject was broached, the more momentum it gained. Finally, eight days after the fine-creating game, the Richmond Braves Players Community Action Pool was presented to the public during a hastily called press conference.

The plan unfolded thusly: Instead of having to foot the penalty all at once, the Richmond players went to a local bank and borrowed $4,500, with the note payable September 1. In the meantime, the R-Braves would attempt to accrue money through the sales of T-shirts, bowlathons, car washes, youth clinics and other fund-raising events. Any deficit still outstanding on the first of September could be garnered by the players from three paychecks instead of one.

The distributed press release stated further that, "Fans and friends of the team can help by: 1. Calling in with suggestions and invitations for fund-raising activities; 2. Contributing to the C.A.P. (Richmond Braves Players Community Action Pool) by stopping in at the Summitt Avenue Branch of Crestar Bank."

Few questions were asked of the players during the 15-minute gathering. However, the R-Braves had no more than departed the bank before the howls began. "How can the players expect the fans, among them young kids, to pay for their wrongdoings?" was the general consensus. *The Richmond Times-Dispatch* was particularly critical. Columnists throughout the newspaper fired missiles, including one by sports editor Howard Owen, who wrote, "Everybody knows the rules, but that doesn't matter...If you don't like the rules, just fall down and throw a fit. Maybe they'll make an exception." The editorial page added its two cents with a cartoon depicting a weaving R-Braves bus that had been pulled over by a police officer. The caption, emitting from the bus, read, "We'll just get the fans to pay."

Noticeably absent throughout the two weeks of verbal banter were the voices of Little and Bruce Baldwin. When asked about the players' efforts, both men reiterated the plans without any perceptible support or defense. The entire mess had turned into a public relations nightmare, and Little and Baldwin wanted nothing more than for the situation to blow over.

"Some days the suspensions hurt us worse than other days," said Little, hoping the topic of conversation would change. "This is something that's written in black and white and you got to go by the rules. We broke the rule, so we have to pay. It's like getting a traffic ticket; you have to pay."

Baldwin waited a week into August before making a public comment about the ongoings. The general manager's message focused on the money raised to date, about $600, adding that half of all donations received would be given to charity. The amount failed to increase above the initial level by the September 1 deadline. The bowlathon featured problems with the alley's contact and wound up attracting only a trio of day-care groups, who all received free autographs. The dealer turnout at a card show was so limited that it failed to generate any income. In the end, each player had to hand over nearly all of the original $300 fine.

"I think it was totally blown out of the water by some people," Mordecai said later. "I'm like any other ballplayer. I did something wrong and I expected to pay the consequences for it. My wife and I were in the situation where we could have paid the $300 and it wouldn't have been a problem. But some of the other guys were not in that situation. They needed some time to come up with the money and it was just best if we took a loan out and paid all the fines at one time.

"As for the criticism, if you didn't like what we tried to do, then you didn't have to participate in any of the things that we were doing. As for the players, I don't think anybody expected the fans and some of the writers to get the idea that we wanted the fans to pay for it. That totally wasn't the case. The entire thing was incredibly ridiculous."

Back on the field, the R-Braves' fortunes were a little more successful than their fund-raising efforts. Richmond overcame its nightly shortage of players to win five of its final nine games in July and finish the month 4½ games behind first-place Charlotte. The team also cleared another brief hurdle when it lost Woodall, who was called up to the Show to pitch the second game of a doubleheader in St. Louis on July 22. Employing primarily his change-up, the left-hander hurled six innings during his major-league debut, allowing five hits, two of which cleared the wall, and three earned runs. He also singled in his first at bat, stroking a clean hit to left field off veteran Rick Sutcliffe. Despite his strong showing, he was tagged with the loss in the Cardinals' 3-2 win.

A day later, following his return to the R-Braves, Woodall's smile stretched across his face nearly as far as the brown-and-black bead necklace around his neck. He had done his job; Atlanta's hitters had not. His taste of major-league coffee had been sweeter than orange juice, without even a hint of bitterness.

"It was a great experience, the best baseball experience I've had," Woodall said. "I was nervous at the beginning, and what I was happy about was I got better as the game progressed. In the last three innings, I pitched better and better. In the last inning, I felt as good as I had the whole game. I felt strong. I got a couple of guys out in key situations; that made me feel a lot better.

"Now I just want to get back up there. Before, I didn't know what I was missing. Now that I know, it's only increased my drive to get there that much more."

The Consumate Professional

16

Brad Woodall's one-night stand in the majors meant that Mike Birkbeck was once again overlooked, bypassed and snubbed by the Atlanta front office. His record stood at a respectable 8-4, with the R-Braves providing just four runs of support in three of his defeats. But in spite of his nearly two years of service to the organization and his past pitching experience in the majors, Birkbeck received nothing more than another indication of just where he stood in the eyes of the decision-makers.

"Mike just has to continue doing what he's doing," Grady Little said. The skipper avoided eye contact; his embarrassment regarding the situation was apparent. After a short pause, Little continued, a little more matter-of-factly.

"He's doing the best he can, and he has to continue to go at that pace and hope he gets the right breaks and the opportunity. You know, once you get to the point where you're doing a job that may be good enough for the major leagues, you just have to wait for that opportunity. It may be that the opportunities we're talking about come with somebody else. If that's the case, it'll be good for him. Either way. But the organization knows that Mike Birkbeck is here. They know what he can do, and they feel good about it."

Most players in Birkbeck's shoes would have been crazier than a fish in a car wash. If the right-hander's heart held any malice, if his mind-set was on the brink of flipping and flopping, in no way was it apparent. He instead further revealed his multilayered makeup, much like an onion, only not bitter at the core. In fact, the veteran had matured to a point where he was simply glad to see someone, anyone, overcome the overwhelming odds and taste the majors, even if it may have come at his expense.

"If a guy's doing real well and has earned it and deserves it, I don't care who it is, I'm happy for him," Birkbeck said after completing his running in between starts in late July. "That mobility re-energizes the club. The guys know they have a chance. I'd like to see everybody get a chance."

The wheels were turning in Birkbeck's mind. He sat silent for a moment or two, something he does habitually during conversations, ignoring the beads of sweat that trickled down his slender face, including one after another off the tip of his nose. "Anybody that plays this game at this level who doesn't think they should be in the big leagues, something's wrong with them," he began again. "They shouldn't be playing. You got to want to get to the major leagues. If you're happy being in Triple-A, you're going to stay there. Something has to motivate you. It's not the money anymore, it's not the bright lights. The major leagues, that's the ultimate, that's where it's at. There's no comparison between Triple-A and the big leagues, and there shouldn't be, really."

Comparisons between Birkbeck's pitching and those performed nightly in the Show produced results that were not near as vast as the differences between the majors and minors. No, Birkbeck, despite a lingering groin injury, a sore knee, an equally sore shoulder, and other vexing ailments that commonly afflict professional athletes at age 33, was putting together a season better than the one he had in 1993, the year he wound up earning a spot on the Braves' 40-man roster. He was once again Richmond's workhorse, taking the baseball every fifth day and nearly always keeping his team in the game.

To measure Birkbeck's contributions just on the days he climbed the hill would be shortsighted. He admitted he did not try to be a leader on the team, but the right-hander quietly helped his fellow moundsmen if the opportunity presented itself. No one had benefitted from the veteran's wisdom more than Woodall.

"Mike's my favorite pitcher ever," said Woodall, his sparkling blue eyes revealing that his adulation of Birkbeck bordered on idolization. "I've learned so much from him over the past year and a half, just talking to him and watching him pitch. He's a bulldog out there. He might not go out there as healthy as everybody else or with the best stuff, but he is so tough mentally. He knows so much about the game. I'm always asking him about certain situations, how to throw to certain people. There's no doubt that he knows more about pitching than anyone I've ever talked to."

Birkbeck at work is a picture of deliberateness. When on the mound with the bases empty, he stands erect, his sloping shoulders perpendicular to the plate, his feet close together and pointed forward. Prior to every pitch, he stretches both arms skyward, eliminating potential resistance from a tucked-in uniform or long-sleeved undershirt. After receiving the sign from his catcher, his body coils into action, his hands chest-high, nearly touching his raised left knee. Should runners inherit the bases, his body turns and becomes parallel to the batter. His glove is face-level, hiding his right hand, which coddles the baseball. Either way, he drives toward home with momentum garnered from his right leg, then unleashes the ball with every morsel of energy his body has to offer, pitch after pitch, start after scheduled start.

His innings pitched stats always exceed 150 during healthy minor-league seasons and provide further proof that Birkbeck is a warrior. His pitch counts are typically high, and he will usually surrender a half-dozen or so hits every outing, with practically every safety a single. He survives by keeping batters off-balance and off-stride with a mixture of pitches: fastball in the mid-80s, curveball, change-up, slider, even a palmball.

Birkbeck acquired the finer points of pitching during his dozen seasons in professional baseball. He also discovered the coarser elements of the game, among them the politics and agendas of his major-league employers. Birkbeck is nobody's fool; he refuses to kid himself. That would lead only to heartache and frustration. He knows as well as anyone that his presence in Richmond is one of an insurance policy, for the Braves, not for himself. And his understanding of the situation without question makes the entire ordeal tolerable.

"I went through a period of time where I was a little bit in a fog about the way the last six or seven months transpired," Birkbeck said. "There were still some question marks about (Steve) Avery's health in Atlanta early on. Other possibilities got me off-track mentally. But I think since the third week in April, I went into my bottom-of-the-ninth mode. I try to pitch every inning like it's the bottom of the ninth. Whatever it takes to get them out, I do it until Grady says that's enough for tonight."

Another pause. "You know, to be honest, when I look at the transactions in the *USA Today*, when I see a guy get called up to the bigs, I might feel a little something that says, 'I wish that was me.' But I don't think there's anything wrong with that. It's not like I dwell on it. I've got a job to do here. You can't concern yourself with everything that's going on because eventually that will take away from what you're trying to get done.

"I learned a little while ago that you have to be able to honestly evaluate yourself. You have to look at the whole situation. Maybe you're not as good as that guy. That's why I don't worry about what they do with anybody else. I got to keep care of my job. The best way I can do my job is to stay within my limitations, pitch like I can pitch. If somebody thinks that I can't pitch, I can't change that. That's when you really get in trouble. You just got to do your job, go out there every day, and rip it."

After another pause extended longer than normal, Birkbeck was asked if he felt at least some frustration with the situation, knowing that he was pitching better than many hurlers at the major-league level, yet still not getting a chance to fulfill his goals. After all, the sand was quickly escaping from his hand and, as far as other organizations were concerned, landing on the wrong end of the hour glass.

"Not really," Birkbeck said after giving the question his full consideration. "I've never found the grass to be greener on the other side. I could become a free agent, sign somewhere else, and be right back in the same situation. At least right now I can say I'm stuck behind the greatest pitching staff on the planet. I could be somewhere else and they might not be as good and everyone might think that I'm a bad pitcher. Just because I'm not in the major leagues doesn't mean I don't have a lot of respect for the Braves organization. I respect a lot of people I don't necessarily like.

"The Braves did what was in their best interest regarding my situation. I don't blame them for that. I learned a long time ago not to get involved in personnel moves. That's their business. I wasn't totally surprised they put me on the roster because I did have a pretty good year. I guess they must consider me to be a pretty good pitcher. So it was a good business decision on their part. And that's their job. Unfortunately, I don't think a lot of the players understand that the front office's business is to protect their team. They may not do what's necessarily in your best interest."

From being drafted by the Brewers in 1983 to reaching the big leagues in 1986 to bouncing to the Indians and Mets organizations and now to the Braves, Birkbeck landed where he did every season because that was the place his employer felt he could best contribute. If any other reasoning had been applied, the pitcher was not aware of it, and would be as shocked as he would be disgusted if he discovered the truth to be otherwise.

That understanding did little to satisfy his desire to ply his skills in the majors. Birkbeck could in many ways relate to the artist who considers his talent as much a curse as a blessing. However, unlike many supremely talented individuals, the pitcher also received more than his fair dose of desire and drive. That's why he continued to choose to separate himself from his wife, Suzanne, and 2-year-old son, John, for half of every calendar year. The money helped, but at this point in his career it was entirely secondary. He had become a prisoner of his dreams, yet he neither asked for nor wanted any sympathy. Birkbeck admitted the bottom line centered on the fact that he chose his course. He made the decision regarding his career and gladly lived with the results.

"When I first signed when I was 22, I never saw myself doing this, pitching in Triple-A at age 33," Birkbeck said. "I totally expected to be very successful. But to be perfectly honest, I probably sidetracked myself throughout my career. I think that's what maybe motivates me a little bit right now, to maybe sneak some time in that I would have gotten before if I would have done my job a little bit better and taken a little bit more pride in it. I took a lot of things for granted, which, when you're young and healthy and you've got a good arm and you're doing well, is easy to do.

"But I continue to do it because I make a good salary here. I still enjoy it. I don't know why anyone would stop doing something they enjoy. I don't care how old you are. It's still a challenge. I go out there and play against guys that are 12, 13 years younger than me."

Birkbeck's discourse was interrupted by a question. Does he ever feel old in the clubhouse?

"I really don't because I think being around younger people keeps you a little bit younger," Birkbeck said. "It keeps you motivated. When you get to the stage of your career that I'm in, you have a certain responsibility to the game to set a good example for the younger players. I remember being around guys when I was younger that were maybe at the same point I am now, and they were bitter. They weren't having fun. I just don't think that's a good kind of player to have around."

His dream and ambition naturally came with a price. Birkbeck is the first to admit that his dedication to baseball causes him to miss many wonderful aspects life has to offer. Foremost in his mind is the event that took place on June 9, 1992. Suzanne, who was at the couple's Canton, Ohio, home, called her husband, then toiling for Tidewater, at the Royce Hotel in Scranton, Pennsylvania, at six in the morning. She was going into labor with their first child.

As soon as he hung up with Suzanne, Birkbeck began making calls to the airlines. Two daily flights departed Scranton for Canton, the first having just left at six, the second one not until four that afternoon. Suzanne's birthing coach, there because Birkbeck was not, kept him updated until the contractions became more frequent. Finally, a phone system was hooked up in the delivery room, and the pitcher listened as the newest Birkbeck, John Laurence, was born at two o'clock that afternoon.

Five hours later, Birkbeck was back pursuing his dream. He took the mound against the Red Barons and almost suffered an arm injury during a scuffle with Wes Chamberlain, who did not care for the pitcher's inside tosses. "I felt good, and I wanted to pitch well. I had that extra adrenalin running that night," remembered Birkbeck, who left the game with the score tied at 2-2, then joined his wife and child after catching the early flight the following morning.

In the 25-plus months since John was born, Birkbeck has been able to spend most of his time between September and February with his family, then settling for sporadic visits during the long spring and summer days. He admits that leaving home is much more difficult than it was when he was younger. Still, he has a talent that earns his family a comfortable living; he has a gift in which he refuses to waste even the smallest amount.

"I've learned that I get paid to be away from my family," Birkbeck said. "I miss my family. There's no question about it. The older you get, the older everybody else is getting, too.

"How much longer am I willing to do this? Till the hitters tell me it's time to stop. The hitters will let me know when it's time to quit. I mean, I don't want to pitch until my arm falls off. But you get a pretty good indication when they start hitting the ball off the boards consistently."

Birkbeck will most likely continue to be a father by proxy for six months of the year if his performance to date continues. He entered his August 6 start against Pawtucket with a 9-5 record, having won only two of his last nine outings, dating to mid-June. Yet those numbers were deceiving. Of his seven winless contests, he left two games with the lead, another was tied and the R-Braves were shut out in two others. A prime example came against Tidewater on July 31, his last start. Birkbeck surrendered two first-inning tallies before shutting out the Tides the rest of the way. Nevertheless, he was hung with the loss in Richmond's 2-0 defeat.

Against the Red Sox in early August, the right-hander continued to gut it out on the mound, the only uncharacteristic aspect of his performance being the season-high three walks he surrendered in the first two innings. Birkbeck was saved by double plays in both instances. In the third, he retired the side in order with a routine shortstop-to-first base ground out sandwiched in between a pair of strikeouts.

However, during the final at bat of the visitors' half of the third, Birkbeck became upset when home plate umpire Rick Roder allowed Jose Munoz time to step out of the batter's box even though the pitcher was in the middle of his windup. Next pitch, Roder called Munoz out looking at a fastball, yet an argument began as Birkbeck walked off the hill. The two combatants exchanged a commentary that lasted less than 30 seconds, long enough to have third baseman Jose Oliva try to convince Birkbeck to continue moving toward the dugout and plenty of time for the pitcher to make some derogatory comments about Roder's ancestry, which resulted in Birkbeck's first ejection since 1988.

"I asked him if he wanted to go out to dinner. I guess the answer was no," Birkbeck said. The pitcher was obviously annoyed by the situation and did not want to discuss the matter further until he offered, "I just wanted to see what the problem was and get it out of the way. I was mad that he let Munoz step out, but then he started yelling at me before the next pitch. It's ridiculous. The umps can do anything, but they won't even let you talk to them. They're horrible. They're all jokes."

Richmond went on to lose that game as well as the next, when Woodall fell to Pawtucket, 13-5. The second loss marked the sixth straight setback and 11th of the last 13 games the R-Braves had suffered at home, leading radio broadcaster Bill Roth to say, "The Braves are celebrating their 10th anniversary at The Diamond by losing all their home games."

As far as the team was concerned, the losses came at an especially inopportune time because first-place Charlotte had hit a bad streak of its own and the R-Braves had failed to take advantage. The Knights held a six-game lead on August 7, a number that dropped to 5½ games on Monday, when the R-Braves' Kevin Lomon shut out Pawtucket, 6-0. On Tuesday night, versus Syracuse, Birkbeck took the mound again after his abbreviated Saturday night stint. Roder was again judging the right-hander's pitches, and Birkbeck was able to record his 10th win of the year by limiting the International League's best-hitting club to three hits over six innings before Brian Bark and Brad Clontz combined to throw three frames of scoreless baseball in Richmond's 5-0 win.

Little walked by and patted Birkbeck on the back as the pitcher sat in the trainer's room, icing his right arm. The skipper made his way back to his office to begin his nightly game report for the Atlanta front office. Little, as well as every other manager in the organization, was required to fax a form containing brief comments on how every player performed, ranging from a few words ("Caught one just right for a three-run HR") to a little more insight than what the numbers indicated. ("HR left park in a hurry; got himself out three other times.") At the end of the sheet, a space is available for the skipper to make some additional comments, ones that typically indicate the mood of the team. ("We had several opportunities but failed to get the runners in; defense has been good; pitchers are working ahead for the most part.") Tonight, the Richmond manager knew what he wanted to write, and needed only a minute to think about how to express his thoughts.

"They're fighters," Little said before sending a similar report to Atlanta. "Birkbeck, Mordecai, Kowitz, practically every one of 'em. They don't leave nothing in the clubhouse. They come on the field and they're going to do everything they can to beat somebody."

Little squinted at the box score before cracking a smile that revealed overall pleasure rather than momentary laughter. "I've never been as proud of a ballclub as I am of this one," the silver-haired skipper said. "I've managed a lot of teams. The fact is, we probably won't have as many off this club go on and play in the major leagues as some other clubs I've had. But this has probably been the most fulfilling team I've had yet."

Lake Luther Williams

17

The rumbling thunder heard in the late July day discharged not from the joining of railroad cars over the right-field fence of Luther Williams Field but from the threatening clouds arriving from the southwest corner of the Middle Georgia city. While the noise may have temporarily quieted the sparrows that inhabit the venerable ballpark, it only turned up the volume from newly bearded Ed Holtz.

"Any asshole in this city could be a weather forecaster," Holtz grumbled as he peered skyward. "A slight chance of afternoon thunderstorms, my ass!"

Holtz's feelings were understandable. The past four weeks, and some might argue the entire 1994 season, had been among the most demanding and certainly one of the more uncertain periods of the general manager's 32-year baseball career. His team had not played a home game in Macon since July 3, and it appeared at a glance that the trend may continue on this Friday evening.

As fate would have it, baseball was played as scheduled on the evening of July 28. Even though Savannah spoiled Macon's homecoming by touching pitcher Jamie Howard for four earned runs in $3^{2}/_{3}$ innings of work in the Cardinals' 6-2 win, the mood was upbeat on the home side of Luther Williams Field. A return to normalcy and stability, as much as can be had in the minors, was again within reach. Since the beginning of July, the team had been on a 26-game road trip, operating out of one low-cost motel after another in a string of humid Bible Belt cities in between bus rides that seemed as long as a Thanksgiving sermon.

In the early days of the campaign, Leon Roberts had said that players at the low Class A level had to be mentally tough, warriors. The Macon manager no longer wondered if his players had the necessary makeup to overcome nearly any challenge. The Braves had survived the worst start in all of professional baseball to finish the first half with a respectable 28-41 record. The second half so far had been even better. After beginning the second season with a 9-3 mark, the Braves hit the road to Spartanburg and Fayetteville and won seven of eight. By the time the team was originally scheduled to return home, it stood alone in first place, having won 15 of 18 outings.

"I think it's been one of the great turnarounds in minor-league baseball," Roberts said. "I told them that things would get better. I don't know whether they believed me or not, but I could see some positive things happening in all that struggle. I could see the guys gaining experience, playing with more confidence, keeping their enthusiasm and competitiveness up. Good things happen when a player and a team does that. It's been a drastic, good turnaround, and the credit goes to the players."

His words aside, without a manager of Roberts' patience, the Braves would have washed away like a sand castle before the surf. Nearly every player credited the skipper and his positive, supportive approach with the team's reversal. Presented with his players' theory, Roberts shook his head, then shrugged before adding some insight.

"I learned a lot from my dad," Roberts said. "I saw my dad get mad maybe one time the last forty years I knew him. I watched my dad work in a paper mill, seven days a week, ten to eighteen hours a day. He'd just grind it out. And when his workday was done, he never griped, bitched or moaned. He picked up the pieces the next day and went to work. He was the boss, the head foreman, a pipe-fitter, and he did that day after day for thirty-two years. You learn things from watching someone like that.

"And there we were at a baseball game, going through a tough time for twenty days. I'm thinking, shoot, in the scheme of things, my dad can grind it out and keep his patience and keep his strength and his workload up and not bitch and moan. He just kept grinding and charging and supporting his family. Here we were in a three-week tough time. You can feel sorry for yourself or you can keep getting after it. You just try to keep your head and your composure and your game plan and believe in your players.

"Tough times make you tough. You appreciate the tough times that give you a backbone. Now we're on a roll. The guys are still getting after it. You got to grind it out a little bit more, and they know that now."

While the players had weathered the storm during the first half of the season, Holtz and the front office had not begun to learn what it was like to fight the elements. The process started shortly after the Braves left Macon following the July 3 tilt with Augusta. The rain was initially hard though intermittent. By Wednesday, July 6, the situation had grown serious. The Ocmulgee River, which flows only a couple hundred yards from the ballpark, began to spill over its banks. A levee broke shortly thereafter, and Bibb County officials

Rising floodwaters from the nearby Ocmulgee River turned Macon's Luther Williams Field into a lake during the early part of July 1994. (Photo courtesy of Macon Braves)

were on the telephone at six in the morning with Holtz, telling the general manager he had 10 minutes to get everything out of the ballpark.

"What can you get in ten minutes?" Holtz reminisced a few days later. "We were able to make sure the uniforms were safe, but that was about it. We had bats in barrels and we thought they were safe, but the barrels floated and tipped over. Even a freezer six-foot tall by five-feet wide floated. Tickets and files and all sorts of souvenirs were ruined. The force of the water was amazing."

Lake Luther Williams was five inches deep upon Holtz's arrival, a level that increased more than two feet over the next several hours. The field, two months earlier one of the smoothest and more lush surfaces in the South Atlantic League, was hidden beneath a sea of thick, muddy water. A bullpen bench, made of heavy wood, floated from the far side of right field to the opposing bullpen along the left-field line. The outfield fence warped and pushed inward, destroying many advertising signs. When the water level finally dropped a day or so later, a 25 pound carp laid to rest in left field.

The losses accumulated. Holtz estimated the damage at $25,000 in inventory alone. More than 175 dozen new baseballs and 15 dozen bats were now waterlogged and worthless. Boxes of peanuts, cases of replica caps, carpet in the modest offices and clubhouses, exercise equipment, a pair of washing machines and a dryer, good only in the dumpster behind the facility. Things that could have been salvaged had the mud been quickly removed were lost due to the lack of clean water. It would be nearly two weeks before water

A boat was needed to get to the iron gates of Luther Williams Field after constant rains flooded the Ocmulgee River in early July 1994. (Photo courtesy of Macon Braves)

service was restored at the park and throughout most of Macon. All the team's officials could do until then was to begin reordering supplies and ready the rubber boots and gloves.

Macon's players and coaches kept abreast of the situation via television newscasts and periodic telephone calls with Holtz. An off-day was slated for July 12, following the series at Fayetteville, but exactly what direction the team bus would be pointed was not certain until Atlanta and league officials determined that the four-game series versus the Charleston Wheelers would take place in Greenville Municipal Stadium, home of the Double-A G-Braves.

"I guess we ought to be careful what we wish for," Danny Magee said shortly after the Macon club left the bus and entered its temporary home. "Everybody on the team wishes they were playing in Greenville. Now we're here!"

With the G-Braves on the road July 13, Macon played a doubleheader on Wednesday before taking part in afternoon tilts the following two days. The upstate South Carolina weather, though dry as a Southern Baptist picnic, was unrelenting during the team's visit. The humid air that made breathing a chore created a sauna effect during the evening's twinbill, a 2-1, 7-0 sweep for the Wheelers. A day later, at high noon, the players baked like brownies in the hazy sunshine. The conditions evidently caused the Macon bats to wilt, resulting in a 4-1 Charleston win on Thursday.

The players soon began to feel the effects of the nomadic lifestyle. Even Leon Roberts found himself suffering from the rigors of barnstorming before deciding the glass was indeed half-full.

"It's like the movie *The Man Without A Country*," Roberts joked. "We feel like a team without a home field. But stuff like this happens and we're much more fortunate than some of the things that have gone on in Georgia. Every one of us is healthy, and we're not scrambling like some of the people in Macon and Albany and Bainbridge."

Moods improved on Friday, July 15, when the aptly surnamed pitcher, Maurice Christmas, ended Macon's three-game losing streak by tossing a four-hit complete game in the Braves' 4-1 triumph. After the contest, the team bus finally headed south to Macon, where the players returned to their apartments, discovered whose cars had been broken into during the flood, washed some clothes, then traveled north a day later to Chattanooga. With Albany flooded more than Macon, and since Richard Holtzman owned both the Polecats and the Double-A Lookouts, the Albany team was able to shift its games to the Southern League city. This time, the Braves adjusted to the Class AA facilities and took three of the four contests.

The Macon schedule was printed in red, depicting home games against Columbus on July 21-24, but the Braves were not on their way back home after visiting Chattanooga. Water service still had not been restored in Macon, forcing the Braves and their next opponent, the RedStixx, to play the four games at Columbus' Golden Park. The two teams split the four meetings, then the Braves headed to Charleston, South Carolina, where on Tuesday, July 26, Macon beat the RiverDogs to even their season record at 51-51, no small feat for a team that once stood 1-19. The Braves also held a 23-10 mark in the second half entering their homecoming contest with Savannah, the first-half Southern Division champions.

Yes, nearly everyone was sporting a smile at Luther Williams Field on this Friday evening. The threat of rain having rolled down the river, Holtz seemed relieved and rejuvenated, so much so that the blown cooling system in a water fountain near the concession stands created no more than a "we'll-get-it-fixed" shrug. The white and gray whiskers on his face served as a time line as to just how long it had been since the Braves had played a home game. During the early days of the flood, Holtz, along with fellow front office employees Jim Tessmer, Brad Cork and Terry Morgan agreed that they would not shave until the team took the field in Macon. All but Holtz, who decided he liked the new look, would soon find a razor and return to their previous grooming habits.

The sight of baseball on slightly damp grounds may have brought the biggest smile to the face of groundskeeper George Stephens. The umpire's bellow of "Play ball!" meant that Stephens could rest his legs for a few minutes for the first time in 12 days. Stephens and his five-man staff had overcome nearly every curveball Mother Nature had thrown their way. A mudslide, which sent 10 tons of infield dirt through the dugouts, down the concrete halls and into the clubhouses before trying to exit via the already clogged drains, had presented the most problems. Considering that a few weeks ago the elevated stands were the only indication that a diamond rested below the water, Stephens' work was nothing short of a miracle worker.

"I never thought I'd say it, but I'm glad to be back in Macon," said John Knott. "You come back and see what some people have gone through and you realize that we were pretty lucky with our situation. It could have been a lot worse. We really had it pretty easy compared to what many people went through."

Knott's change of attitude entering the final month of play had been as dramatic as the team's fortunes. Success does that to a player. The third baseman had chipped in with his share of production, succeeding at the plate more than 27 percent of the time and pacing the team with a dozen home runs and 30 stolen bases. His defense had also met the standard at the hot corner, leaving Knott comfortable with his production, even if he still longed to be in Durham.

"I sat back and realized that ever since I was a junior in high school, I wanted to do this," Knott said. "I love to work at it. People say baseball's work, but to me it's fun. It's always been fun for me, and it's always been a dream. There might be guys that are more talented than me, and there's nothing I can do about that. But I can certainly work as hard or harder than anybody else. I made a little vow to myself that I'm not going to be outworked by most guys."

In spite of his recent success during his second stint in Macon, Knott still felt the burn of not being promoted to Durham, especially now that the calendar read August. The stinger was still lodged in his skin, irritating him to no end, making his whole body angry and upset if he thought too long about it. Had he been drafted, particularly in the first 20 or so rounds, his cap would sport a Bull instead of "Macon" and a tomahawk. That fact was always just below the surface of Knott's feelings, ready to erupt if roused.

Exactly why Knott wanted to go to Durham centered on his competitive drive, a trait that had as much to do with his, as well as every other professional athlete, earning a paycheck every two weeks from the parent club. Even if the move would not prove beneficial, Knott longed to right what he felt was a wrong.

In reality, Knott's cause was being helped by remaining in Macon. Had he jumped to Durham, he would have revisited the same situation he endured

Carey Paige received what every minor-leaguer hopes for — a midseason promotion. (Photo by Action Sports Photography)

throughout the 1993 season. Robert Smith was the anointed third base prospect at the Class A level; Knott was little more than a roster-filler, no matter his production. Were he in Durham, he would be right back on the bench, watching games, taking BP and doing little else. And no player ever impressed the decision-makers while riding the pines. At least in Macon he had the opportunity to make a statement with his bat and the numbers it produced.

"I think I'm having the kind of year they didn't expect me to have," Knott said. "Nobody expects much from undrafted free agents. My attitude has been like it's always been. Just work hard and be glad I'm doing this and not in the real world. I'm living a dream right now. Even though it's the minors and it's Macon, it's still a dream."

Unlike Knott, Macon's top two starting pitchers had recently experienced upward mobility. Roger Ethridge joined Durham on July 11 after going 3-1 with a 3.55 ERA in seven outings for the Braves. Carey Paige, the team's most consistent starter, followed a couple weeks later.

There was no denying Paige's accomplishments during the first four months of the 1994 season. An intimidated young man who realized that he pitched not to lose instead of to win during his first two seasons as a professional, the right-hander had matured physically and mentally during his 20th summer to emerge as a prospect in the eyes of the Atlanta front office. His 8-6 record in 19 starts did not begin to reveal his progress. His 1.70 ERA, 119 strikeouts and only 87 hits allowed in 105.2 innings were the numbers that spoke volumes. His lone stumble had been a sore shoulder, acquired while sleeping on a lumpy mattress during Macon's homeless stretch, which caused Paige to miss a couple of starts in mid-July.

"I've discovered that every time I go out to pitch, I'm still learning," Paige said. "I'm learning about the hitters. I study what I do wrong and what I do right. Every outing I go through is a different level. I just keep going at it."

Paige had also succeeded in spite of a family problem back in Abilene, Texas. His grandmother, whom he had been close to during his childhood, had been sick throughout much of the season. The pitcher spoke frequently with his mother on the telephone, receiving updates on his grandmother's failing condition. Finally, at one-thirty on the afternoon of July 26 in Charleston, South Carolina, the telephone rang in his Howard Johnson's Riverfront room. It was Paige's mother. "It's time to come home now. Your grandmother only has a few more days."

Paige agreed, for he wanted to be there to pay his last respects when the time came. After hanging up the receiver, he started planning his course when the telephone rang once again. Roberts was on the horn. "I need you to come down to my room," said the manager.

"I was real nervous, kind of scared," Paige said. "I thought my mother maybe didn't want to tell me something, so she told Leon."

His hands twitching and his pale blue eyes blinking more than normal, Paige walked down the hotel hall, knocked on his manager's door, and walked in. The pitcher didn't say anything; he just looked up slowly at the huge manager, only to see a smile across Roberts' face.

"Congratulations," Roberts said, his hand extended toward Paige. "You're going to Durham."

"I couldn't believe it," Paige said. "I mean, I wanted to get called up, but I had given up on getting promoted this year. It was getting late in the season and I had heard through the grapevine that they weren't going to make any more changes. I was focused on finishing the season out strong and helping us reach the playoffs. It was definitely a day where I felt all the emotions, both good and bad."

One emotion Paige felt was one that few players ever experience and even fewer admit. He wanted to move up and prove himself at the next level, yet he also felt the desire to help finish what the Macon team had started.

"I hated to leave Macon because we were doing so well and headed toward better things," Paige said. "Don't get me wrong, I wanted to get promoted, but I also wanted to help us win in Macon after all we'd been through there.

"Now I'm putting everything I did in Macon behind me. This is a different league with different and better hitters. I don't know if Atlanta just wants me to get my feet wet for next year, but hopefully I'll do well enough to get to Double-A."

It was suggested that once he reached Greenville, that is, on a full-time basis, he could be just a phone call away from the major leagues.

"Yeah," Paige responded as his mind started to drift at the thought. "Things really start moving then."

Movin' On Up

18

Larry Rothschild did not crack a smile beneath his straight blonde hair, but his feelings were clear about the progress Carey Paige had displayed so far in the 1994 season.

"He thought about being a third-round pick too much," said the roving pitching coach after yet another session of instant therapy with another minor-league hurler. "It bothered Carey. He's a young kid with a lot of talent who wanted to do well. When he didn't, he tried to get it all back at once and became scared. It looks like he's gotten over that now, because he did not have one bad game at Macon."

Having been on the road to Damascus, Paige's pause in Macon preceded the journey to Durham. And because of his rapidly improving ways, prosperity continued for the pitcher during his initial start with the Bulls. Although he was a little rusty due to his absence in lieu of his grandmother's death, the right-hander tossed five shutout innings at Winston-Salem and picked up the win the first time he took a Carolina League mound on August 7. His fastball showed good movement, and his change-up was a little high, though nothing he was unable to overcome. His Durham teammates contributed with their biggest outburst of the year, a 15-run barrage that included six roundtrippers sailing out of the bandbox that is Ernie Shore Field.

Helping support Paige was the home run bat of Tom Waldrop. Contrary to Paige, Waldrop's boat had traveled a stormy sea in 1994, the waves ejecting some of the outfielder's one-time supporters and leaving the player more than a little sick to his stomach.

It was not that Waldrop hadn't tasted some success. He had, enough to put together a pretty decent highlight reel, in fact. His torrid hitting streak in late April and early May, his high-voltage power explosion during the Fourth of July weekend, and the only two grand slams the team had produced through the first week of August were accomplishments that had made the campaign memorable. At the same time, those streaks created even more frustration for Waldrop when his bat grew quiet, either through his own failure or the decision of Matt West and the Atlanta front office.

Said Waldrop, "We've had a lot of outfielders here, and they tell me I'm fine. But you can't do much when you're not playing." Which had been the case lately. With Damon Hollins holding down center field, both on merit and the Braves' request, Mike Warner, the Carolina League player of the month for July, playing regularly in the outfield since fully recovering from an injury in mid-June, and Miguel Correa laboring in left most every day since his demotion from Greenville on May 20, Waldrop and Juan Williams were left to battle for any crumbs that remained, such as designated hitter or a rare start on the lawn. The stats accurately told the story, with Waldrop hitting a mere .223 with a relatively impressive 11 home runs and 43 RBIs.

The silver lining could be located in the fact that Paige filled Warner's roster spot after the latter was promoted to Greenville on August 3. One less outfielder meant more playing time for Waldrop and Williams, which proved to be the case on the evening of August 8, when Waldrop was listed as the Bulls' right fielder against Wilmington.

Durham entered the game having survived a win-one, lose-one streak for the past 10 days, and remained atop the Carolina League's Southern Division standings by six full games. The team was living in large part on its one impressive stretch of the season, from June 27 until July 8, when the Bulls triumphed in 10 of 12 outings. Helping matters since then had been the consistent pitching of Roger Ethridge, the left-hander promoted from Macon on July 11 who had won three of four decisions over five starts and posted a startling earned run average of 0.96.

On the hill for Durham this particular Monday evening was Mike D'Andrea, a right-hander with a 9-7 record. The weather, unseasonably cool with low humidity, did not give the pitcher the boost such a night normally provides hurlers. D'Andrea looked tired through the first three innings, his change-up failing to hit its intended spots. As the game progressed, his location improved to the point where he was able to keep the team in the game for eight complete frames before handing the ball over to Carl Schutz.

"Felt like shit, didn't have anything in the beginning," D'Andrea said after his 24th appearance. "But I got better as the game went on. I felt better at the end than I did at the start."

The previous season, D'Andrea's first full slate of his career, he started impressively with a 5-0 record prior to faltering toward the end and crawling to an 8-7 mark at Macon. The primary reason, said the pitcher, centered on his failing to take proper care of his body. As Ken Giard and several other players discovered the hard way, the 1993 Macon club thrived on late-night toddies. D'Andrea was still not above making an occasional trip to the trendy college bars the Durham area offered, although he believed that a little more restraint had made a difference come the early weeks of August.

"For me, the season is starting to get long," D'Andrea admitted. "But if you work out hard in the off-season and eat right all the time, those are the keys."

That approach is difficult to follow during the season. More often than not, the bus stops at some fast food hovel between cities, with the team's trainer or driver having to talk the restaurant's employees into producing another batch of hamburgers and fries after closing time has come and gone. The dining choices are only a little more varied once at the hotel. Without any transportation other than their feet, the players are at the mercy of the immediate surroundings.

Having not played as much as he was accustomed, Waldrop disagreed that the schedule was beginning to take its toll. His feelings definitely lodged in the minority, Waldrop's pregame positiveness centered on the fact he was in the lineup for a second straight game. Yet, once he began swinging the bat in competition, his rustiness showed.

In his first at bat, in the third inning, Waldrop watched a fastball from Wilmington's Mike Bovee tail outside for a ball. He then fouled the second pitch, a curveball, against The Dap's wire backstop. Bovee then offered Waldrop a change-up, low and outside. The left-handed hitter bit and missed the toss badly. One and two. Another fastball landed outside the strike zone, a ball, before a third heater split the plate in two. Waldrop was frozen by the pitching exhibition. Expecting an off-speed pitch, he was completely off-balance and could not react when the fastball approached at 90 miles per hour.

"I don't know what he was looking for to take a pitch like that," said one scout, sitting behind home plate.

"He must have been guessing the whole way," added another.

"Vapor lock," offered a third.

Waldrop did little to redeem himself in his next two at bats. A weak ground ball to second resulted in another easy out in the fifth before the outfielder went down swinging in the seventh on a breaking ball, low and away. With three weak efforts in as many tries, Waldrop could feel the mounting pressure to produce. His playing time already limited, he had less than four weeks to salvage what had been a difficult campaign.

The Bulls owned a 3-2 advantage at the end of eight innings. The Blue Rocks threatened to touch D'Andrea in the top of the frame, only to have the third out recorded when a Wilmington runner was nailed at the plate on a strong throw from the outfield by Correa. Despite having little of his typically vast arsenal, D'Andrea had fought tooth, fang and claw, surrendering just two earned runs while scattering 10 hits.

The Bulls failed to dent the scoreboard in the home half of the eighth. West decided D'Andrea's night had run its course and turned the pitching chores over to the erratic Schutz. The hard-throwing lefty led the team with 13 saves, but had blown nearly half as many, as evidenced by his 4.57 ERA. The trend continued on this evening, with the Blue Rocks' Lance Jennings crossing the plate on a two-out wild pitch to tie the score at three apiece.

Though the scouts had departed to a local taproom, the game's conclusion had not been reached. Returning the favor Schutz offered in the top of the inning, Wilmington third baseman Steve Sisco could not handle a hard-hit grounder by Hollins, who wound up at second on the two-base error. Standing in the on-deck circle, stroking the resin towel along the handle of his black wooden bat, Waldrop studied the situation like Bobby Fischer perusing a chess board. Standing on the mound was right-hander Jim Chrisman, meaning the matchup, right-handed pitcher versus left-handed hitter, leaned in Waldrop's favor. Nevertheless, with a potential "o-fer" staring him in the face, Waldrop hesitated ever so slightly before making the short walk to the batter's box, hoping that West did not call him back to the dugout in favor of a pinch hitter.

West never whistled. Waldrop planted his left foot in the dusty hole at the rear of the batter's box, his stance slightly open, his bat cocked and twitching tenuously toward the top. Chrisman twirled a fastball, right down the chute, not unlike the one Waldrop admired for a called third strike in the third inning. Waldrop was ready. His right foot stepped into the pitch, his shoulders and hips followed through and turned, creating power at the most prosperous moment. Waldrop's contact crushed the ball, drilling the sphere over the first baseman's head and down the right-field line. Hollins easily galloped home with the winning run while Waldrop was greeted with pats on the back from his elated teammates.

It took nearly 10 minutes for Waldrop to work his way through the adoring crowd and into the Bulls' tiny clubhouse in the far back corner of The Dap's bowels. Fans of all ages, who took advantage of the 20-foot walk players had to make between the field's surrounding chain-link fence and the off-limits area that begins at the bowels' entrance, waited for Waldrop's signature on programs, scorecards, caps and cards. Despite his desire to get showered and on his way, Waldrop could not refuse even the least-prepared children. As far as the outfielder was concerned, the price was a small one for such heroics, feats that had been too few over the past 4½ months.

"That hit made the game a lot better," Waldrop said after showering. "At the very least I wanted to get Damon over to third. But the pitch was right there, and I turned on it."

Registering the deciding tally was as beneficial to Hollins as recording the hit was to Waldrop. His statistics revealed that his production had been much more consistent than those of his fellow outfielder, but Hollins had recently experienced one of the first slumps of his fledgling professional career. Stuck on 19 home runs over the past couple weeks, the center fielder finally reached the magical 20 mark by chipping in with one of the six long balls on Sunday at Winston-Salem.

Privately, the Atlanta front office was delighted to see Hollins struggle. The Braves believed that Hollins would learn from his difficulties, much as he had earlier in the season when the outfielder was allowed to skip Macon and begin the year at Durham. As the youngest player in the Carolina League, Hollins faced pitchers who on average had three or four years experience under their professional belts. The hurlers held the early advantage, but once Hollins saw their stuff during his first time around the circuit, the tide turned, and the 1992 fourth-round draft pick quickly showed why Appalachian League managers rated him the top prospect in 1993.

"It was very tough to start the year here," Hollins said. "Looking back, I think it was all in my head. The pitchers were a little bit older here, but I finally realized that even if I had gone to Macon, they would have been older there, too. I just had to get settled and make that adjustment."

As the adjustments were made, primarily because of the outfielder's indubitable tenacity, Hollins' stock as a prospect continued to solidify. His strength had even added to the lore of The Dap, where the 5-foot-10, 180-pound right-handed hitter drove a ball in batting practice through a wooden fence sign toward the base of the right-field wall.

"I didn't even know it had happened until a day later," Hollins said. "A guy on the grounds crew came up and told me. I came out and took a look and said, 'Wow, I did that?' I couldn't believe it, although that day in BP I was hitting the ball pretty good."

The lone flaw Hollins had revealed also involved his bat. His average dipping to .270 was of no concern; his 96 strikeouts were. He had not learned to be patient every time he stepped in the batter's box, which again divulged his age as much as anything else.

"I think as far as the Braves are concerned, they want to develop players," Hollins said. "Sometimes that means putting a player where they might struggle. I understand that. After the spring training I had, I think they were confident that I could swing my bat up here. And I knew there was no question that I could play at this level. Now that I've begun to come out of my slump, I think I can finish the year and prove them right. I just gotta keep swinging the bat well and stay healthy."

The Monday night win also brought a smile to the face of Pete Anlyan. "There's nothing like winning," beamed the general manager. "It's not the most important thing, but it sure doesn't hurt when you hear on television, 'The Bulls won another game last night and are well on their way to the playoffs.'"

Much of Anlyan's time in recent weeks had been devoted to various idiosyncrasies involving the construction of the new Durham ballpark. By mid-August, the facility was recognizable, and the early reviews had been nothing short of rhapsodizing. The general manager was obviously anxious to begin play in the yet-unnamed stadium, even as sentiment regarding The Dap still flowed. Some of that sentiment oozed from a cynical press, much of it based nationally, that continued to harbor on the perceived embarrassment the Bulls supposedly felt over having to market the "second final season" at The Dap. Nothing was further from the truth. Some of the badmouthing had affected attendance, however, which was down more than 40,000 from the same point in 1993.

That was about all that had changed. The fans were still having as good a time as could possibly be had at a ballpark. Anlyan had pulled no punches in acquiring the best promotions the minors had to offer. Giveaways were practically a nightly occurrence, ranging from thermal mugs and kids' jerseys to seat cushions and miniature bats. The Phillie Phanatic made a mid-July appearance. Anlyan even hired The Famous Chicken, who earns a six thousand-dollar check every time he performs, for two different dates. Top that off with some good and improving baseball from the Bulls along with a plethora of concessions, and a trip to The Dap proved nothing short of being the quintessential minor-league experience.

"I think that entertainment is entertainment, and this is sports entertainment," Anlyan said. "And this is family entertainment. If somebody comes here and has a bad experience, they may not come back, either here or at the new place. So we need to make sure the folks are going to come out and not only see some good, clean fun out on the field, but the whole family is going to enjoy every aspect of their visit. That includes the food, the souvenirs, the accessibility and the affordability of all that. That's a very big factor. When they walk back out that gate, are they going to be smiling or are they going to be shaking their heads about what a terrible time they had? We want to send them away smiling and, of course, we want them to come back. In that aspect, it's like a lot of other entertainment industries.

"Basically, I think if you can sell, then you can sell baseball. If you can market, then you can market baseball."

19 An Audience in Chattanooga

Three and a half hours prior to game time on August 18, the seats of Chattanooga's historic Engel Stadium held just two spectators while the homestanding Lookouts took batting practice. The two onlooking men, both clad in white golf shirts and khaki pants, were recognizable to just about anybody who followed major-league baseball. Yet, since the setting was Double-A and a time of year when pennant races were normally beginning in the majors, Bobby Cox and John Schuerholz looked as out of place as a couple of nuns in a singles bar.

Up until seven days earlier, there had been the makings of a pennant race in the major leagues. Cox's Braves had played well for most of the season. And although Atlanta trailed streaking Montreal by six games in the National League East, it seemed likely that the Braves would clinch nothing worse than the wild-card spot for the expanded playoffs.

That scenario was quashed when the clock struck midnight on August 12. For the eighth time since 1972, the players went on strike because of lingering labor negotiations. That left fans without the game at its highest level and Cox and Schuerholz with little to do other than to see what the minor leagues had to offer.

"Damn this place is great," Cox said while surveying the patriarchal brick stadium, circa 1930. "They've really done a good job here. Last time I saw this place, must have been at least 10 years ago, it was a shithole."

Engel Stadium had experienced a couple of major renovations since Cox's last visit, the grandest taking place prior to the 1990 campaign. The ballpark underwent a facelift costing more than $2 million. Improvements were made to the field, green awnings were attached to the brick facade, wrought iron was added to the front gates, antique lamps decorated and lit the grounds. The remainder of the facilities were either power-washed squeaky clean or exchanged altogether.

Cox and Schuerholz were not the only members of Braves management in Chattanooga. With the Lookouts hosting Greenville, Atlanta pitching coach Leo Mazzone and dugout coach Jim Beauchamp arrived just prior to the visitors' batting practice. Dressed in their road Atlanta uniforms, the two major-league coaches were there to offer their assistance to the Double-A players. Whereas their plans called for a 12-day stay with the G-Braves, their lifestyles would not become minor-league during that time. Greenville public relations assistant Sean O'Connor made the trip from South Carolina to give the two coaches their major-league meal money, a total of $1,400. Mazzone and Beauchamp also would fly from Chattanooga to Raleigh instead of having to suffer for 10 hours to Carolina on the team bus.

The presence of the major-league officials was noticed by every member of the G-Braves. "I don't think you play any harder because they're there," said Tim Gillis, who would strike out, pop up to second and ground out later that evening. "You can't play this game very well if you're not relaxed. But you do hope you do well. You never know when you might do something that might catch someone's attention."

Deep down, Gillis knew that it would take the hand of fate to make an impression on the front office in 1994. Other than a torrid streak in late June, the third baseman had struggled for much of the campaign. His numbers, a .244 batting average, nine homers and 46 RBIs, held little attractiveness. Any appeal his consistency at the plate had produced had vanished over the past week, a seven-game stretch when Gillis was mired in a 2-for-26 slump.

"I think everybody comes into a season wanting to have a career year and this hasn't turned out to be the one for me," Gillis said. "I'm not disappointed with the way I'm playing or with my effort. It's just that sometimes I didn't get the results that I want. As far as my effort and everything, I'm happy with it. But statistically I would love to have a better year."

Improving Gillis' approach had been the team's performance. Late July was kind to the G-Braves, who won 10 of their last 12 games of the month to move into first place in the Southern League's East Division. An August 3 win over Orlando and a three-game sweep of Birmingham had solidified that spot, so much so that Greenville still held a two-game advantage over Jacksonville after dropping five of its last eight outings.

"We're in the pennant race and that's a driving force every day," Gillis said. "You go out and want to win. That's the way you approach it. Honestly, you don't even think about it being August. You know you only got a few games to go and you want to click it in and finish up really strong. When you're not playing for a pennant race, it's a little tougher.

"We're a pretty streaky team. Baseball is streaks, peaks and valleys. You just hope your peaks are longer than your valleys. That's the name of the game, consistency. You aim to be consistent and get to the playoffs and play for something at the end of the year. That's what makes the season."

Were it not for the possibility of earning a spot in the playoffs, Gillis admitted that he might give more thought to his status in the organization. Idleness provides time for the mind to wonder. In professional baseball, the long bus rides and the endless nights in ammonia-cleaned motel rooms offer an opportunity to reminisce and to wonder what might have happened.

Gillis could easily ponder what might have happened this year had he been sent to Richmond instead of taking one for the team and reporting to Greenville. What if he had gotten off to that fast start? What if he had remained at third base, a position where he was rated the organization's best defender in 1991, instead of moving across the diamond to first in 1993, only to shift back to the hot corner because a teammate was inept everywhere in the field but would cause the least damage at first base?

"I try not to think about it," Gillis said. "I just want to go out and play hard and just see what happens. I have confidence in my abilities, but you never know. You don't know who's watching or seeing you and thinking that you can play or thinking you're the worst person to ever put on a uniform. You really can't concern yourself with the exterior factors of the game. The only thing you can control is that day and break it down to that play or that pitch."

Some players on the team, almost to a fault, could not help but think about their future. Tony Graffanino had done little to hurt his status as the next second baseman in Atlanta's plans. After bobbing around the .300 level for much of the season, he had slumped to .270 before rebounding of late to enter the game in Chattanooga hitting .288, tops on the team.

Among the G-Braves' position players, Graffanino was considered the top prospect. Other teams also recognized his status, leading more than one general manager to telephone Schuerholz in hopes of trading for the second baseman. The loudest rumor circulating before the players' strike had Graffanino and another player headed to the Chicago Cubs in exchange for closer Randy Myers. The strike quieted such scuttlebutt, yet Graffanino wanted to know if anything else might be in the works.

"Chicago would be a great place for you, Graff," said Kevin O'Connor, who in addition to being the team's resident card had also become the most improved center fielder in the Southern League. "Those fans would love to have a wop playing second base for them."

Grinning at the comment, Graffanino responded, "It doesn't matter to me which uniform I'm wearing. Braves, Cubs, it doesn't matter as long as I'm in the big leagues."

Circulating rumors did not focus solely on the field personnel. Chuck LaMar had been mentioned in recent weeks as a potential general manager candidate for the Cubs and the Texas Rangers. Driven in the same vein as players such as Graffanino, LaMar's goal was to reach the highest level his profession offered, and at age 37 with a string of success stories in three organizations, LaMar appeared to be on the verge of taking over the day-to-day operations of a major-league club.

Further rumors persisted that even Schuerholz, the man credited with the tremendous turnaround the Braves had experienced since his arrival in 1991, would fly the coop to the Orioles. Schuerholz began his baseball career in Baltimore, and many believed the general manager would welcome completing the circle before he retired. An article in the *USA Today* he was holding said as much, even though Schuerholz, unbeknownst to those sitting around him at Engel Stadium, had earlier that day signed a contract extension that would keep him in Atlanta as executive vice president and general manager through 1999.

His status solidified, Schuerholz made some mental notes that night in Greenville's 10-0 victory over Chattanooga. Starter Chris Brock rose to the occasion by contributing as much with his bat as with his arm. A former outfielder at Florida State who pitched just one game in college, Brock evened his won-lost record at 5-5. Batting because the opposition was also a National League affiliate, Brock took Marcos Vasquez's offering over the fence in his first at bat, short-hopped the left-field wall for a double in his second trip to the plate, hit a pitch down the line for a single in the fifth and added another single in the seventh to finish the game 4-for-4 with three runs scored and three RBIs. He was just as adept on the mound, allowing just three hits over seven shutout innings.

Equally pleased that night was Matt Murray's soon-to-be grandfather-in-law. Murray's fiance, Nikki, and 14 family members traveled the 50 miles from Calhoun, Georgia, to Chattanooga to cheer the G-Braves. Murray did little other than throw on the side before the game and sit in the dugout. That was fine with the grandfather, who, according to Murray, was "happy as a pig in shit" that Cox was sitting one section over in Engel Stadium.

The colloquialism also would have adequately defined Murray's state of mind in mid-August. The right-hander stood 3-3 with a 4.03 ERA since his June 28 promotion to Greenville. More importantly, his velocity had improved since spring training. Throwing in the low- and mid-80s in West Palm Beach, Murray had been clocked as high as 93 four days earlier in Jacksonville. He was also snapping off his curveball without fear of wrecking his surgically repaired elbow. Even his change-up, long a pitch he had been unable to master, was showing signs of significant improvement.

Murray's disposition had changed with his rediscovered success. Earlier in the year, the always-affable pitcher became withdrawn. Much of that seemed to border on embarrassment, caused strictly by the way he was pitching. If not for the help of Nikki, his parents and his priest, Murray's right arm might have been pushing a pencil in a college classroom in late August instead of throwing a baseball.

"There was a time in May when I wasn't really sure I wanted to play," Murray said. "I'd given up twenty home runs in ninety innings and I just thought maybe it was time to quit. But I had always said to myself, 'I'm going to play as long as they'll let me. As long as they give me the ball every fifth day, I'll take it.' Nikki gave me a lot of support and just said, 'Do what you want to do. I'm sure you'll probably regret it if you don't keep seeing what happens.' From that point on, I've just started to say, hey, if it doesn't happen, it doesn't happen."

That attitude also helped Murray's mental approach regarding his arm. For all his progress over the past two seasons, there were many instances when the right-hander would fail to put his entire body into a pitch. He would hold back without realizing it. Something deep in the back of his mind kept telling him to be careful; he had blown out his arm once, it could happen again.

"I'm finally getting to where I'm over that," Murray said. "I mean, sometimes I feel like my elbow is stiffening up. That's kind of scary. Or I'll turn a door knob and feel a little twinge and start worrying. Thank God there's been no problems really to speak of. I think I've come to realize that if I do my exercises, that's all I can really do."

Every evening, either in his motel room or apartment, Murray follows a strict exercise program of stretching with some rubber tubing, designed to build the muscles and keep the pressure off the replaced ligament. Murray then grabs a 10-pound weight, performing biceps and forearm curls. The entire process takes approximately 30 minutes, time that must be made in order to give himself every opportunity to succeed.

Despite his dedication, the exercises seemed fruitless during April and May. Greenville loomed as an impossible destination for Murray. His efforts finally started to show on the mound, and since his arrival at Double-A, he had shown flashes of brilliance regardless of an overall lack of consistency from start to start. He won his first outing, a one-run, five-hit affair on June 29, then was bombed for 12 hits and seven earned runs during his second Double-A contest, at Knoxville. His next seven games had been competitive, with his best performance, reminiscent of the Murray of old, coming on July 28, an eight-inning, four-hit, 10-strikeout effort at Nashville. That start, as much as anything, proved to the pitcher that Nikki had indeed been right.

"At times I feel like I'm moving along here," Murray said. "My arm's back and everything, and I have come a long way. My arm has been healthy, which is a big positive. I've made all my starts. But then again there are some nights when nothing seems to work. At this level, you can really see the difference. You have to throw at least two pitches for strikes if not three. I've even struggled with my control and that's one thing I've never done.

"It's all a matter of keeping the confidence between every start. The thing that I've done well is battle and keep the team in the game. There have been situations, like second and third with one out, where I haven't allowed a run to score. I guess that's what I'm most proud of."

As hard as it was for Murray to believe sometimes, the 1994 season was the first year since 1990 that he had pitched from start to finish. His surgery and long rehabilitation required the 1988 second-round draft pick to readjust his timetable in reaching the majors. Whether he attained that level with Atlanta was becoming more uncertain by the day. He remained on the 40-man roster, but Murray was also out of options. That meant if he was not protected that winter or did not make the major-league club next spring, he would have to clear waivers, making him available to any other organization. Nevertheless, Murray focused on the task at hand instead of worrying about the future.

"All my friends are here, the Braves have stood behind me, and it's a great organization to be with," Murray said. "It's not the greatest organization in terms of moving up due to the pitching staff in the major leagues. But it's getting to the point where something is going to have to happen, to have all these prospects and nowhere to go. I know they've had a lot of confidence in me to have stuck by me through the surgery and everything.

"I really don't know what's going to happen. I know that I'm healthy, and I know that whoever I'm with and wherever I'm at next year, I can help the team and make it with someone. It's obviously in the back of my mind. That's the crazy thing. Nobody knows, maybe not even the Braves at this point."

The Dog Days

20

Former San Francisco catcher Bob Brenly once said, "By the end of the season, I feel like a used car." The Macon players who did not require at least a tune-up during the latter weeks of August needed a complete overhaul. Whether it was the forehead full of red pimples caused by a summer's worth of sweat beneath their wool caps, the slow-paced jog between workouts prior to games, or an inability to reach balls that could have been outs in May, the Braves were obviously dragging in what was for many the conclusion of their first full season in professional baseball.

"This is the time of year when you separate the men from the boys," said the always-intense Larry Jaster, Macon's pitching coach. "When they report here in April, the pitchers are usually ahead of the hitters. Then the hitters catch up in June and July, when the pitchers begin to feel some of the wear and tear on their arms. That's why August is the survival of the fittest. Those guys who eat well, who work hard in the off-season, those are the ones who succeed and make an impression on me."

August is also the time of year when players begin to procure a pretty fair read on their progress. Most do not need to see a scout's evaluations or hear from the front office. The players' attitudes will typically be revealed on the field. Those wanting to put the crowning touches on a solid year will continue to bust it until the final out registers. Others who are disappointed will usually end the season poorly by making mental errors, their heads wondering what the future holds instead of whether the runner might take the extra base.

"This last month has really been hard on me," said Danny Magee. "I thought I was ready to play a full season, but I realized I should have been in better shape because I've been dragging a little bit. I'm giving it my all to make it through the day, then I'm spending the next day doing the same thing. I think my bat speed has slowed down. I'm seeing the pitches and hitting them, but I'm getting jammed and beaten back a lot. I got to really power to get the ball out there. It's really catching up with me. I'm losing weight, playing out in the heat every day. I hope we finish up strong, then I can go home and relax."

Magee was one of several Macon players who will return home knowing that his future is brighter than when the season began. In many ways his year mirrored that of the team. Magee started slow for the first few weeks before he made the necessary adjustments. By June he was taking shape as the best shortstop prospect in the organization. Now that the calendar read August, his batting average was consistently at the .270 mark, an excellent figure for a player batting eighth and ninth in the lineup and whom the Braves believed might never hit with consistency.

"Earlier in the season I was trying to make too many plays," Magee said. "Instead of just keeping balls deep in the hole, I was throwing it and sometimes throwing it away. Now I've matured and I'm more experienced about some of the plays. I know when to throw it and when not to throw it. I've learned a lot. All things considered, I think I'm getting there."

The shortstop had also matured thanks to the help of Roberts. Nary a day passed without the manager amiably needling Magee.

"You're still in preschool," Roberts told Magee. "You think you've had a good year, but you're a kindergartner. You know how you only go to school for half a day in kindergarten? That's you until you prove you can finish this year."

"I got two hits last night," Magee tried to retort.

"You call those hits? Was your mother keeping score last night? One of those weak-ass grounders barely reached the outfielder. The other, if you were playing in Texas, you'd just go back to the dugout, knowing you didn't deserve it. But if you want to live with those, that's your choice. I guess that's what we get for drafting a guy from Louisiana."

Regardless of Roberts' tongue-in-cheek remarks, Magee had played a major role in the team's impressive turnaround. After the game on August 19, the Braves stood 35-19 in the second half, had won seven of their last 10 and held on to first place in the Southern Division by one game over Columbus.

The most recent victory came on the previous evening in Columbia, South Carolina. Macon defeated the Bombers, 11-0, with Jermaine Dye bringing home a half-dozen tallies on two roundtrippers and a double. If anyone had proved himself as a prospect on this Class A team, it was Dye. But the entire team had come to the forefront over the course of the season, causing others in the league to take note.

"They've made adjustments to the league," said Capital City manager Ron Washington. "They've got some good athletes, some kids in the outfield who can run the ball down. And all through the lineup, they're getting hits. Everybody is supplying help. When you get that, you can win."

Also supplying help was John Knott. The third baseman gave Macon an early lead against Capital City with his team-leading 16th home run of the season, a long blast over the left-center field wall in the top of the third that looked as if it would hit the full beige moon hovering above the Bomber Bowl. Knott's batting average had climbed to .288, while his 36 stolen bases and 72 runs batted in ranked second on the club.

Angry for most of the first half, Knott seemed to have finally accepted the fact that he had spent two full years in Macon. Happy with his production, he tried not to look at his statistics. Of course, every week or so, Knott would see the stat sheet laying around and could not help but take a peak.

"I'd like to think that I'd be in Durham right now if we weren't in the playoff race," Knott said. "But then again, I hit .280 and a high draft pick hits .280, he'll go up and I won't. I understand that, even if I don't agree with it."

His understanding increased with indications nearly every day of exactly where he stood in the organization. In addition to not receiving a promotion, he had been snubbed by the front office regarding his request to play winter ball. He had heard in the meantime that a couple of his higher-profile teammates were slated to play somewhere during the off-season. The lack of attention and respect obviously irked Knott.

"I want to do anything to prove whether I can play this game or not," Knott said. "It may be the end of the season, but I'm still ready to go. All I want to do is play baseball. Twenty-four hours a day would be great to me. I just want a chance to prove myself."

Knott's fervor, if not so rabid, would have been dashed two nights later. Following a much-appreciated off-day on August 21, the Braves continued the eight-game road trip against the second-place RedStixx. Once the Monday evening affair concluded, the teams were tied atop the Southern Division after Columbus took a 10-9 decision.

Macon then fell out of first on Tuesday night because of Columbus' 9-7 triumph. The RedStixx lead increased to two games on Wednesday and to three games on Thursday, when Columbus completed the sweep of the tetrad contests. Instead of taking the typical route and demanding his players respond to the challenge of a pennant race, Roberts simply encouraged and reminded them of how far they had come over the past four months.

"Leon remained calm and told us all to stay focused," Magee said. "If we turn around and win this, he'll be the reason why."

"Why ride them or yell at them?" Roberts said. "They tried hard and played hard and made some mistakes. You can't fault the effort. We're busting our rears; it just didn't happen the way we wanted it to."

Roberts' approach had been consistent throughout the season. He treated his players as professionals and they, in turn, responded in a mature manner beyond their years. Only once had the skipper's actions bordered on those of a baby-sitter. On August 11, Roberts entered the Sports Spot, looked at his watch, and noted it was ten till one in the morning. He walked over to the carousing players and said, "I know all you guys will be in your apartments by one."

Curfew was one o'clock, but it had not been enforced all year. The players later said that Roberts' actions had been the result of a mandate from members of the Atlanta front office, many of whom were in town the previous week.

Rules enforcement was far from Roberts' mind upon making the 93-mile journey across two-lane highways back to Macon. Instead, the manager was concentrating on the challenge his team faced. The Braves returned to Luther Williams Field to play nine of the season's final 10 games. A good showing during that stretch and the result could be what many once thought impossible.

Attendance had increased in Macon since the major-league strike began two weeks earlier. Atlanta played a small role in the boost by allowing fans who held major-league tickets to cancelled games to enjoy general admission seating for free and box seats for a dollar. And unlike other teams across the minors, Macon was allowing the fans to keep their tickets so the patrons could send them to Atlanta and receive a full refund.

"We're seeing about twenty-five to thirty Atlanta tickets a night," said Ed Holtz. "I don't care if it's the same people every night with one ticket as long as they're coming in."

His beard a reminder of the flood, Holtz leaned back in his squeaky, brown office chair. To say the least, the 1994 season had been challenging. The team's poor start and the subsequent negative reaction from the public and the local press, the constant rain and flooding, the repairs and physical labor required to keep the stadium operable, all combined with the typical bugaboos that a minor-league team operator must encounter was enough to make Holtz as happy as many of the players that the curtain was about to drop on the campaign.

"I thought I had seen it all until this year," said Holtz, smiling at his naivete.

Holtz had steered minor-league teams during strikes at the major-league level. In early August, the general manager believed that because of Macon's proximity to Atlanta, the strike might actually help his club, if for no other reason than the public's insatiable desire to watch professional baseball. And that had been the case. However, by the final days of the season, Holtz was beginning to feel the baseball backlash during the luncheons and other functions he regularly attends throughout the Middle Georgia community.

"I tell them, 'Don't take it out on my players, who are only making eight hundred and fifty dollars a month. For chrissakes, we travel in a damn bus up and down the Eastern Seaboard.' I agree, it is getting ridiculous, this whole strike business. But they shouldn't take it out on these Class A players," Holtz said.

Another aspect had made Holtz's season more difficult. Negotiations regarding an extension of the working agreement between the city of Macon and the Atlanta front office had taken place for most of the summer. Both sides had been happy with the relationship that began in 1991, but the debate centered on who would pay for what improvements that needed to be made at Luther Williams Field, as per the terms of the Professional Baseball Agreement signed in 1990 between Major League Baseball and the National Association of Professional Baseball Leagues, a.k.a., the minor leagues.

The agreement, which the National Association's members were strong-armed into signing, contains countless and many ridiculous measures, yet none affects small-town America as much as the requirements for the minor-league teams' facilities. Renovations and even rebuilding are required of nearly every ballpark, with a completion due date of April 1, 1995. The conditions range from the number of urinals in the men's restrooms to mandates on seating capacity, parking spaces, individual locker size and umpire facilities.

On the field, there are standards for lighting, dugout size, foul-pole length, even the mandatory addition of a clock that must be visible from both dugouts. The hundreds of demands have left operators of even the newest facilities scrambling, with taxpayers having to shell out hundreds of thousands of dollars just to keep professional baseball in town. A 65-year-old stadium such as Luther Williams Field, meanwhile, could become as obsolete as a slide rule, with an estimated $500,000 worth of upgrades required to keep it operational under terms of the PBA.

Officials representing the Atlanta Braves and Macon city officials started negotiating in February. Progress had been made, but not without a little posturing. According to the current contract between the team and Macon, the city guaranteed the sale of 275 season tickets. Mayor Tommy Olmstead had said that the city was not in the business of selling tickets, and even if it was, then the Braves should guarantee a certain number of victories and not the "embarrassment" that took place earlier in the season. Chuck LaMar bristled upon hearing that comment.

"We're in the business of player development, and no one is going to dictate to me how to run my organization," LaMar said. "We're not going to put one game or anything else ahead of the development of a single player. We will never be concerned about a win or a loss at any of the minor-league levels. That only damages the development of a potential major-league player.

"Let me add this. There are a lot of baseball fans in every city throughout the Southeast that would love to have their team wearing Braves uniforms."

An agreement between Macon and the Braves would finally be reached in the early fall. Whether it had anything to do with the final nine games of the regular season is doubtful, although the home team did provide the city's fans with a fair share of excitement prior to the long winter's nap.

Jermaine Dye, who earlier in the day was named to the South Atlantic League's year-end all-star team, proved again he deserved the recognition with a three-run homer in the first inning of Macon's 11-2 win over Albany on August 26. Combined with Columbus' 4-3 loss to the Charleston RiverDogs, Macon trailed by just one game in the standings. Macon's 10-7 win against the Polecats followed on Saturday, along with a 6-2 victory, paced by three RBIs from Randall Simon and a solo homer by Knott, on Sunday afternoon. The Braves then made it four straight over Albany with a 9-0 triumph on Monday night to remain one game behind the first-place RedStixx.

The sweep demonstrated once again the recognizable change in the Macon players. No longer did they have the deer-in-the-headlights look. No, this club had become the hunter instead of the hunted. They wore their battle scars like a badge of courage and knew that on most nights they were the better team, no matter what had taken place in April and early May.

Macon took a half-step closer to a championship on Tuesday night, August 30. While Columbus was rained out against Augusta, Simon continued his scalding ways by depositing a change-up over the center-field wall for a three-run homer. That dinger highlighted a six-run first inning and guided the Braves to a 17-2 win over the RiverDogs. On Wednesday, Wonderful Monds, who two weeks earlier had to plunk down $15 at the souvenir stand for a Macon cap after leaving his team-issued model on the bus, swatted a pair of solo homers to guide Macon to a 2-0 win over Charleston.

Thursday night brought more of the same. Prior to the contest, the Macon Braves Booster Club and Sertoma Club extended their team awards, bestowing the most valuable player distinction upon Dye, outstanding pitcher honors to Esteban Yan and best reliever accolades to Marcus Hostetler. Knott, Andre King and Gator McBride each received $100 from Southern Land and Lumber for hitting home runs over the company's left-field sign during the season. And, in what would up be many of the players' first taste of national television exposure, 16 Braves and several members of the Macon front office were filmed singing *Oh, What A Beautiful Morning* for *CBS This Morning*. Ken Warner won the lead role, shouting "Good morning, Paula!" to show co-host Paula Zahn at the end of the rendition.

Warner then went out and helped extend Macon's winning streak to seven games in front of 2,468 fans who partook in the final "Thirsty Thursday" promotion of the season as heartily as the Braves played on the field. The second baseman doubled home Simon in the sixth with the go-ahead run in the Braves' 4-2 win. Afterwards, Dye appreciated the team award, but his focus centered on the final three games.

"When I think back on this season, I'll remember our comeback most of all," Dye said. "We couldn't do anything about the flood, but we were determined to do something about our performance. We have, and I think everyone here is real proud of what we've done."

Columbus continued to stay one game ahead of the Braves throughout the week, then moved 1½ in front after Friday's play. The RedStixx defeated the GreenJackets, 11-1, while the Braves' game was cancelled after rain soaked the field for two hours, beginning in the second inning. More than 100 fans withstood the elements before the umpires decided at ten o'clock that continuing the contest that night was beyond reason.

Unflinching, the Braves resumed their winning ways on Saturday, defeating Augusta 4-0 behind the 10-strikeout performance of Yan before receiving a standing ovation from the home crowd after the last out was recorded. Word had quickly spread throughout Luther Williams Field that Columbus lost its first game of a doubleheader against Albany. Yet, long after everyone had departed the Macon facility, the RedStixx took the nightcap, 6-4, to remain one game in front with one to play.

The 121-mile trip to Augusta for Sunday's finale did nothing to alter Macon's success. The Braves defeated the GreenJackets, 2-1, ending the regular season with nine straight wins and a second-half record of 45-23, 73-64 overall. A loss by Columbus would result in a tie, with the Braves taking the division by percentage points since they played two fewer games than the RedStixx. The point became moot when the final score from Polecat Park was announced. Columbus had withstood Macon's incredible run and defeated Albany, 8-5, to win the flag.

Initially somber on the way back to Macon, the mood was upbeat once the bus pulled into the parking lot of Luther Williams Field for the final time. The players had no ring to show for their success, but the team had accomplished more than any piece of jewelry could reveal. Ridiculed early in the year, the Braves were perhaps the best team the South Atlantic League had to offer at season's end. Not only had they gone 70-41 after the first 26 games, the Braves finished with a team batting average of .262 and an earned run average of 3.12, both of which placed second on the circuit. More importantly, despite claims from Atlanta that victories were not crucial, the Macon players knew they were winners. And that confidence, combined with their improved skills sharpened in the wilting heat and sodden fields that only the Southeast can offer, could do nothing but cause dreams to continue, for most of the players as well as for the Atlanta Braves.

"None us ever gave up," Magee said. "Even when we were 1-19, we still knew that we could compete with everybody. I think a lot of teams would have blown up and said, 'We just don't have it.' Our young team, we played strictly on adrenalin. We get pumped up and we take every game like it's our last game. I like that. That's why it's fun to play on this team.

"This whole year helped us mature and experience a lot about baseball. I like the way our team came along. I know I'll always remember the guys here. We've been through a lot, and everyone on this team feels like we came out on top. Considering what we experienced, I don't think there's many teams that would have accomplished what we did here."

Dream On

21

The handshakes and slaps on the back were brief in the Macon clubhouse; the good-byes even briefer. Regardless of how successful or disappointing the season had been, every player longed to return home and forget about baseball. Many players departed within a matter of minutes after the bus arrived from Augusta. Others had flights to catch out of Atlanta that would effectively disperse the team to all parts of the country. A few would be back on the diamond in two weeks for instructional league in West Palm Beach, others would return to Florida next spring, the rest would begin exploring other opportunities now that playing baseball would no longer be a paying occupation.

Jermaine Dye thought that he would be back in Vacaville, California, immediately after Macon's season concluded, but that was before the Atlanta front office decided a couple more games might benefit the outfielder. Instead of heading west, Dye traveled one rung and two states north, to Durham, second-half winners of the Carolina League's Southern Division.

Their progress not as pronounced as Macon's, the Bulls had nevertheless quietly put together a nice rebound of their own. After finishing the first half with a league-worst 28-40 record, Durham turned things around, winning the division with a 38-30 mark, 6½ games ahead of Winston-Salem. No part of the club's attack was particularly spectacular, for the Bulls placed next-to-last on the circuit with a .248 batting average and a mediocre fifth in team pitching with a 4.44 ERA. However, having started the year as a group of fragmented cliques, the players grew closer and began to believe in themselves as the days grew warmer. That was accomplished in part because of the constant psychological work of Matt West. The skipper squeezed every ounce of effort out of his team. The result was most obvious in mid-August, when the Bulls won eight of 11 outings to all but wrap up the division crown.

"Matt is an excellent coach," said Tom Waldrop. "There aren't hardly any games, and that's why his best trait is his ability to get players to play for him. It's hard to explain, but he gets one hundred percent out of players who typically give just a seventy percent effort. He really makes guys want to get out there and play."

Waldrop's comments were particularly poignant considering the outfielder was in no way one of the manager's pets. Not to say that Waldrop was in the skipper's doghouse; it's just that he received no preferential treatment when it came time for West to make out the lineup card. The right fielder's playing time had been sporadic all year, inducing a .215 batting average, 12 home runs and 54 runs batted in during 97 appearances. Even if some positives could be extracted from those figures, the season had produced more moments to forget than ones to remember.

No stranger to the politics of professional baseball, Waldrop understood that some of West's decisions to make the player a spectator for more than one-third of the season came from the Atlanta front office. And it was for that reason Waldrop was not shocked to see Dye dressing for the first time into a Durham uniform during the playoffs. Considering what had taken place, it was appropriate, all in the name of player development.

Bud Waldrop also was not surprised about the year-end events. At a price of nearly $300 from Howe Sportsdata, he subscribed to the weekly stats of every minor-league game played in the Atlanta farm system. The father studied the numbers into the wee morning hours on more than one occasion, trying to figure out where his son might stand in the organization's eyes, hoping in the meantime that a telephone call from Durham might bring news that the numbers were increasing in all the right places. That had not happened as often as he would have liked. In fact, Bud was beginning to wonder if his third and final trip to Durham this season might be the last time he watched his son take the field to play baseball.

Other more certain finalities also were taking place. For the second time in as many years, the Bulls and their fans saluted Durham Athletic Park for a job well done. More than 6,600 fans filled the revered ballpark on the Sunday prior to Labor Day to watch the last professional regular-season games played among the water towers and abandoned brick warehouses and factories that comprise one end of downtown Durham. Due to a rainout two days earlier, a doubleheader with Kinston was played on September 4. The Bulls and Indians split the twinbill, with Durham taking the opener, 3-0, and Kinston the afterpiece, 2-0.

Appropriately, the last Bulls pitcher credited with a victory at The Dap was right-hander Jeff Bock. A native of Durham, Bock spent a couple childhood years serving as a batboy at the ballpark when his dad, Pete, was the Bulls' general manager in 1980 and 1981. But the family legacy goes back even further. Bock's maternal grandfather, Buck Weaver, was not only a former Bulls pitcher, he had his ashes raked into The Dap pitcher's mound upon his death in 1962.

"This is a dream come true," said Bock, who had an otherwise lukewarm season, consisting of a 4-8 record. "I spent a lot of time around the park back when my dad ran the team. It's a great place, and I feel real fortunate to have actually played here and played for the Bulls."

A few eyes glistened with dampness on that Sunday afternoon as well as a day later, for the opening game of the best-of-three playoff series with Winston-Salem. The sentiment appeared in many ways to be reserved. Most of the regular patrons had made their peace with the ballpark's demise last year; the 1994 season had been one long thanks-for-the-memories encore that ended more fittingly with a second-half championship.

Hopes of additional games at The Dap quickly faded. With Waldrop on the bench and Dye in right field, the Bulls lost the first playoff game to some timely hits by the Spirits. Roger Ethridge, who sparked the team with his 6-2 record and 1.40 ERA since his mid-July arrival from Macon, was hit hard in the 7-4 loss, effectively deflating the rest of the team, which counted on the left-hander to carry them when he took the mound.

A day later at Ernie Shore Field, the pitching of Chad Fox enabled Winston-Salem to defeat the Bulls, 6-3. Waldrop found his name in the lineup and responded by driving in a run on a single in three trips to the plate. Though downcast over the loss, Waldrop felt satisfied with his contribution. Exactly what the future held from here would not be determined for a couple months.

"Nothing's going to surprise me," Waldrop said. "I'll either get a letter in the mail with an 'X' next to the box saying I've been released or an 'X' next to the one saying where my contract has been assigned. I don't know what's going to happen. Until I find out, I'll just go home, start working hard and hope that there is a next year."

• • •

Strong second-half showings were not relegated to Atlanta's two Class A clubs. Buoyed by one five-game winning streak and a pair of four-game strings in the final 12 weeks, Greenville put together enough solid pitching and the circuit's best defense to go 37-31 and win the Southern League's Eastern Division second half by 3½ games over Jacksonville.

As was the case in Macon and Durham, the manager played a significant role in the team's revival. Bruce Benedict, whom several observers wondered earlier if he was ready to manage at the Double-A level, proved his mettle throughout the campaign. At no time was his major-league catching experience more beneficial than in the final month when he had to overcome the promotions of pitchers Terrell Wade, Chris Seelbach and Brad Clontz. Helping fill the void was Jason Schmidt and Chris Brock, who responded to the challenge and continued to show why the organization considered them prospects.

Benedict's improvements also came about because of some changes in his approach. In 1993, when Benedict began his managing career at rookie-level Danville, the stresses of the job affected his handling of the players. He was respected, but extremely unpopular. In 1994, the skipper learned to take the day-to-day occurrences in stride. He also gave the players a little more breathing room and allowed them to learn from their mistakes instead of insisting that everything be carried out to perfection every day.

As a result, the likes of Jerry Koller, Kevin O'Connor and Pedro Swann made immeasurable strides during the campaign. The same held true for more heralded players such as Tony Graffanino, Schmidt and Brock, along with the foursome who had been promoted to Richmond. As Chuck LaMar constantly reminded everyone in spring training, the Braves were not running a YMCA. Player development was the objective, and it had been achieved in Greenville.

One player whose name Benedict did not mention in his assessment of those making progress was Gillis. Crippled early in the year by batting woes, Gillis had experienced both extremes in 1994, hotter than a fresh tar road in South Carolina at times, colder than a frozen yak at others. Yet, with his positive, team-first attitude, the infielder had played an indirect role in the progress of his contemporaries.

"Tim is and always has been a quality person," Benedict said. "He's just a very fine individual. He's played awfully well for us most of this year, especially at third base defensively. He's done some marvelous things over there. He'll be the first to tell you that his hitting hasn't been where he wanted it to be. He'd certainly like to iron that out a little bit. But for the most part, he's a very reliable player. He's a joy to have on your club. He comes to the ballpark to play every day and conducts himself as a professional. This organization should be proud of Tim Gillis."

No better an example of Gillis' attitude existed than during the division playoffs with Carolina. Most minor-league players care little about the post-season. The Braves do not offer any bonuses, only prorating their salaries for however many days the season is extended. In recent years, particularly at the Triple-A level where players are hoping for a late-season call-up to the majors and a daily salary of $595, participants have been known to throw in the towel, simply trying to end the misery as soon as possible. Nothing could be further from the truth with Gillis.

"When you play this game, you don't get a chance to play for championships that often," Gillis said. "There's some guys who played 10 years and never get to play for a championship at any level. Any time you get that chance, it's a special time. Honestly, this may sound crazy, but that's why I play. I love to play for a championship every year. You play as an individual to play in the major leagues, but along the way, there's the developmental part, too. You can learn to win. When you win championships, that kind of carries over to the next level."

Gillis ended the season in a manner similar to the way he started it. His batting average concluded at .241. He did finish third on the team with 50 runs scored, and fourth with nine homers and 48 RBIs. He admitted that those numbers did not merit the promotion to Triple-A that he wanted. Instead, similar to Tom Waldrop at Durham, Gillis had started thinking about life after baseball.

"I think about getting released," Gillis said. "You never know. For one thing, you could have a good year and get released. There's no guarantees. You never know what's going to happen. And toward the end of the season, you say, 'Man, my numbers are not as good as they normally are. My age is getting up there, too.' You try not to worry about it and just go play, as the old cliché goes, one day at a time.

"I want to give baseball every opportunity I can. I had a coach in college tell me one time, 'Don't ever say you want to play in the major leagues and don't stop until you get there.' That's the way I look at it. There will be stuff to do once I get out of the game. I've talked to some people and they like me. Whenever baseball is done, I'll have some options. But I'm not pursuing those things right now. Everything I do, I try to do a good job at it and work hard. I'm going to play baseball until I can't play anymore."

Not everyone associated with the Greenville club possessed Gillis' enthusiasm. When asked prior to the G-Braves clinching their fourth straight playoff appearance if he hoped the streak would continue, Steve DeSalvo smiled sheepishly and said, "No comment. It's been a long season."

DeSalvo's feelings were understandable, his reasoning two-fold. One centered on the wear and tear everyone in the Southern League felt as a result of perhaps the worst schedule ever concocted in professional baseball annals. Because of the Atlantic Coast Conference baseball tournament in Greenville for a week in May, the World Cup in Orlando during July, and the nomadic Nashville Xpress franchise having to work around the Triple-A Nashville Sounds' games played at Herschel Greer Stadium, the circuit slate had become one tremendous abomination. For example, the G-Braves played at home on August 15, went to Chattanooga and Zebulon for a combined six games, returned to Greenville Municipal Stadium for a scheduled one-game series against Jacksonville on August 23, had two days off, then finished the regular season with three road games each at Knoxville, Orlando and Jacksonville. Such travel patterns caused four of the 10 Southern League teams to vote against the schedule in March. Nonetheless, president Jimmy Bragan, who once said that "my schedule maker could make out an eight-team itinerary in the bathroom," adding that a 10-team league "takes a little more time," could offer no other alternative because of the various cities' peculiarities.

"People here have forgotten about baseball since mid-August," said DeSalvo, beginning his second explanation for his lack of playoff enthusiasm. High school and college football in South Carolina rank, in no particular order, with God and pickup trucks. Once the calendar inches anywhere close to the end of August, all interest is on the gridiron. *The Greenville News* even pulled beat writer Abe Hardesty off baseball and onto football, opting instead to pay G-Braves radio broadcaster Mark Hauser $15 a night to call in the details. For those reasons, along with the ongoing players' strike in the majors, DeSalvo knew he would be lucky to attract 500 people for any September contest.

The feelings notwithstanding, Greenville qualified for the playoffs and traveled from Jacksonville to Zebulon, North Carolina, to meet the Mudcats, winners of the first half. Carolina defeated the G-Braves 13 of the 20 meetings during the regular season, but that trend did not hold water on the first night. Behind the eight-strikeout pitching of Schmidt, Greenville took the first contest, 3-1, before Carolina evened the series a night later with a 6-2 triumph.

The series moved to Greenville, where the G-Braves won game three, 8-1, in front of a reported 1,544 fans that looked to be one-third as many. Brett Backlund knotted the series a night later at two wins apiece by silencing Greenville's bats on four hits in front of an equally silent 775 fans in Carolina's 4-0 win. That set the stage for the fifth and final game, which would enable the winner to meet Huntsville for the Southern League championship.

If any Greenville player had been nonchalant earlier in the series, that was not the case on September 9. The G-Braves sent to the mound Matt Murray, the right-hander who had turned his season as well as his career around since the middle of May. Murray continued to prove his major-league potential, fanning seven Mudcat hitters and allowing only a leadoff home run to Jermaine Allensworth, who entered the game with just one roundtripper all year, through the first six innings. The pitcher then encountered trouble in the seventh, with reliever Tom Thobe providing little help in Carolina's two-run frame. Gary

Wilson and Jeff McCurry, meanwhile, scattered seven Greenville hits for only one run, which allowed the Mudcats to take the game, 3-1, and the series, three games to two.

Afterwards, the Greenville players started putting plans of returning home into action. Disappointed with having lost, Murray took a little extra time disrobing. The reality had hit home. There was a chance, some believed a very good chance, that the right-hander might be taking off a Braves' jersey for the final time in his career.

"There's really not much I can do," Murray said. "You have no control over anything. The only thing you can do is pitch well yourself. Especially with the Braves. It's tough." He stopped, looked around the tattered upholstered furniture in the middle of the G-Braves' clubhouse, then glanced briefly into his small blue locker. "You just have to worry about yourself, keep pitching well, and know that something will happen. Something's going to have to give. As long as I keep pitching well, whether it's with the Braves or with somebody else, I think that something will happen."

Murray's situation was not unlike those of many of his teammates. Durham and Macon both featured a crop of young players that would fill at least half the Greenville roster in 1995. Which of the current G-Braves would move up to Richmond remained to be seen. But that was far from foremost on the players' minds. The immediate future was most important, a time that did not include baseball.

"I am just going to get a job back home and spend some time with my wife," said Gillis, one of the players who appeared most dejected about the playoff defeat, his 2-for-17 batting performance in the series serving as a major reason for his mood. "I don't know exactly what I'll do. I've got some oars in the water. I worked last year at a Pepsi distributor stacking pallets, so that's a possibility. It's a tough job, but it's money. Right now, everything is just kind of a question mark."

• • •

Mike Birkbeck said earlier in the season that he tried not to be a leader on the Richmond club. He denied it again in late August, even though his actions displayed traits of leadership. The right-handed pitcher showed how badly he wanted a championship when he purchased T-shirts for the R-Braves' players and front office staff that read, "Go Hard or Go Home." Those words had been uttered all season by pitching coach Bill Fischer. Now they had become a battle cry for the surprising and overachieving team on the verge of winning the International League Governor's Cup Trophy for the first time since 1989.

"This team has the players to win," Birkbeck said. "Grady has been great to play for. We have the pieces, so why not try to win the thing?"

The unselfish R-Braves had been on a mission all season, hanging close to first place before faltering in early August. But just as it appeared that Richmond's chances of reaching the playoffs were becoming a pipe dream, the team went on a rampage at the right time. In a two-week span beginning August 8 the R-Braves won 10 of 15 games. At the same time division-leading Charlotte dropped 11 of 14, allowing Richmond to slip atop the standings by one-half game.

That lead held tight until the final five-game series of the season, featuring three meetings at Charlotte's Knight Castle, followed by a pair of contests at The Diamond. The major-league strike in full bloom, the players knew that whatever the next few weeks brought would be all the season would offer. Adding a feel of importance was the presence of national television cameras from ESPN2, WTBS and SportSouth, which beamed some added attention to the typically obscure minor-league playoff atmosphere. The Richmond fans also helped create the proper aura with more than 10,000 patrons filling The Diamond's seats in seven of the last eight regular-season home games.

The final series equalled the hard-fought duels the Knights and R-Braves had encountered throughout the campaign. Charlotte won the opener, 4-3 in 12 innings, despite five hits by Richmond outfielder Brian Kowitz. Terrell Wade took the mound a night later and displayed his Double-A form, assuring Richmond of a playoff spot with a beautifully pitched 4-1 win. The R-Braves built their lead to 1½ games by winning 3-2 in 10 innings on September 1, setting the stage for a triumphant return trip home to The Diamond.

Wasting little time to settle the regular-season score, the R-Braves produced champagne-and-beer baths for all on September 2. Tyler Houston, who had just three home runs to that point in the season, began the celebration by driving a Chad Ogea slider over the right-field wall with two outs in the bottom of the eighth to guide the home team to a 3-2 victory.

"I think our ballclub has surprised a lot of people with what they've done," said Grady Little, the International League's manager of the year, as bubbly dripped off the ends of his graying hair. "I think practically every player we have here has given us his very best. We've tried to stress all season long that we want to play this game right. It's kept us in the race. We always go into every season hoping that by the first week of September we have a chance to win. We're now in a position where we have that chance to win it all."

Headaches were prominent a day later in the clubhouse, but the ill effects from a night of celebrating did not prevent the R-Braves from ending the regu-

Mike Mordecai's impressive play at shortstop helped Richmond win the International League pennant. (Photo courtesy of Richmond Braves)

lar season on a positive note. With a record crowd of 12,744 fans shoehorned into The Diamond, Richmond's Anthony Telford felt good enough to register his 10th win of the season, and Terry Clark recorded his 26th save in the Western Division champion's 4-3 win.

Having won four of five from the Knights, the R-Braves traveled back to Fort Mill, South Carolina, to begin the division playoffs. Mirroring the final regular-season series, Charlotte won the first game, 5-1, behind the three-hit pitching of Albie Lopez. Mike Mordecai evened the series a night later when he launched a home run in the eighth inning to give the R-Braves a 6-5 victory.

Mordecai's home run was appropriate in several ways. The team posted wins throughout the season with the help of a different hero every night. Other than the consistent pitching of Birkbeck and I.L. pitcher of the year Brad Woodall, someone new stepped to the forefront when the game was on the line. It was Wade's pitching a week earlier in Charlotte, Houston's home run for the division two days later, now Mordecai's blast to tie the series at a game apiece.

The dinger also was befitting in that Mordecai had gone deep a career-high 14 times during the season. His career total prior to 1994 had been 15 over five minor-league campaigns. In addition, his 14 jogs around the base paths matched the record for an R-Braves shortstop, first set in 1974 by Larvell "Sugar Bear" Blanks.

"I was really surprised at the home runs I hit this year," Mordecai said. "I went through a few times where I got fatigued, but I worked through those. My average fell off toward the end of the season, but I'm back. I think the thing I've been most happy with is the strides I made defensively at shortstop. That's the job of any shortstop, defense, and by adding a little bit of power at the number two slot, I'm just trying to help us do anything to win."

The revolving door of heroes continued in Richmond on September 7. Woodall was his typical spectacular self, allowing four hits and three runs through one out in the eighth. Brad Clontz took over and set down two of the Knights' best hitters, David Bell and Chris Cron, before Pedro Borbon retired the side in the ninth after Richmond's five-run attack in the bottom of the eighth sealed the 9-3 victory.

Two nights later, it was Birkbeck's turn to shine, this time in the opening game of the Governor's Cup championship series against the Syracuse Chiefs. The veteran pitcher breezed through the first two frames at MacArthur Stadium, surrendered a pair of runs in the third, then retired 12 of the next 13 hitters he faced. Mike Kelly padded the pitcher's production by taking the Chiefs' Scott Brow over the left-field wall for a two-run lead in the first inning, then added a bases-loaded double off the fence for two more runs in the second. The R-Braves' relievers performed some damage control in the final two innings to preserve the 8-6 win.

No one admitted it at the time, but something in the teams' approaches let observers know that the series' outcome had been decided that first night in Syracuse. Richmond took the second game, 11-7, with Judd Johnson picking up the win and Clontz the save. Back at The Diamond, in front of 12,103 fans, Woodall shut out the Chiefs for seven innings and Jose Oliva swatted a solo homer in the fourth to give the R-Braves a 2-0 lead after seven innings of play. Clark retired the side in order in the eighth, followed by another insurance run for Richmond in the bottom of the frame.

A buzz emitted from the near-capacity crowd at The Diamond once Clontz, the minors' top closer of the 1994 season, took the mound to open the ninth. The fans' enthusiasm quieted somewhat as the Chiefs created a few nail-biting moments. Carlos Delgado and pinch-hitter Ray Giannelli came through with singles, and Rich Butler walked to load the bases with two outs. The side-arming Virginia Tech product refused to give in. He used the adrenalin rush produced by the standing patrons to coerce Marty Pevey to lift a can of corn to Kowitz, giving Richmond the win and the International League championship.

If winning does not mean anything in the minors, somebody forgot to tell those at The Diamond on September 12. After retiring Pevey, Clontz was greeted by his catcher, a leaping, spread-legged Eddie Perez. The rest of the R-Braves poured out onto the field and became one large pile. The crowd stood and celebrated for more than a quarter-hour. Little received a victory ride on the shoulders of his players, who then began to douse one another as well as Bruce Baldwin, dressed in a pin-striped shirt and tie, with champagne. Holding their arms and the Governors' Cup trophy high above their heads, the R-Braves had accomplished the unexpected. Unheralded to the end, the players pulled together and proved to everyone exactly what they could achieve individually as well as a team.

The celebrating continued into the small hours of Tuesday morning, making the cleanup chores for clubhouse manager Steve Barden that much more difficult. It would take more than a day to cleanse the sprayed alcohol from all the uniforms and T-shirts and off the walls and lockers of the Richmond clubhouse, a chore Barden considered a small price for success.

Exactly where that success would land Richmond's players next year was even more uncertain than the futures of those at lower levels. Everyone wanted a shot in the majors; everyone knew that the limited opportunities would make that possible for only a few. The normal politics of professional baseball were becoming more chameleonic as the players' strike continued at the game's top level. A worse time to be a Triple-A player may not have existed.

Such thoughts did not bother Birkbeck. The right-hander had again put together one of the game's most consistent seasons, winning 13 games, good for fifth in the league, placing second on the circuit with a 2.73 ERA and 28 starts, and fourth with 143 strikeouts. He had chipped in with a victory in the first game of the championship finals, and helped more than one aspiring major-leaguer with the nuances of pitching at the game's top level.

Still, he had not done what he had thought he would, and that was help the Braves at the major-league level in 1994. That shortcoming was not his fault. At least one organization had been interested in his services during the campaign, but Atlanta wanted Birkbeck to remain in Richmond and continue to serve as an insurance policy. The strike commenced soon thereafter, leaving the pitcher with no option other than to lead the R-Braves as best he could.

Not unlike a cowboy dropping opposing gunslingers in one dusty town after another, Birkbeck holstered his belongings in the Richmond clubhouse; he knew not the site of his next confrontations. He did, however, know his desire, and that would remain constant, that is, until the opposition proved to him that it was time to retire his sharpshooter and go home for good.

"To be perfectly honest, I'm going to be in the major leagues," Birkbeck said before returning to Ohio to reunite with his family. "No question in my mind. But I am not the type of guy who wants to be in the major leagues and not pitch. I don't want to be just a number. I want to make a contribution to the team. That's what I felt I did here, and that's what I'll do for somebody up there."

Epilogue

A major-league organization constantly evaluates the development and failures maturing young men in the farm system endure in order to determine what promise they might hold for the Show. Some players originally thought of as long-term projects emerge as prospects and need little more than a princess' kiss to surprise even the most hardened critics and become major-league material. Others, considered princes in earlier times, fail to maintain those handsome traits and turn quickly from prospects to suspects.

Such turns took place within the Atlanta organization over the course of 1994 and into the 1995 season, when the Braves finally attained their long-held goals and won the World Series. Despite the success, changes afflicted the minor-league organization, particularly when assistant general manager Chuck LaMar was named the first general manager of the expansion Tampa Bay Devil Rays in late July of 1995.

"This is a dream come true," LaMar said. "To have an opportunity to build a team from scratch and to work with such a dynamic organization like Tampa Bay is what everyone aspires to do. Men such as John Schuerholz and Bobby Cox helped make this possible, and I'm very excited about getting started."

As far as the primary players (final 1994 statistics are found in parenthesis) mentioned in this book are concerned, they fared thusly:

The two playoff games with Durham at the end of 1994 wound up being all Jermaine Dye (.298, 15 home runs, 98 RBIs, and a league-record 44 doubles at Macon) saw of the high Class A level. Rated the organization's No. 6 prospect, he climbed to Greenville in 1995 and left no doubt that his future is among the brightest in the Atlanta farm system by hitting .285 with 15 homers and 71 RBIs.

Ken Giard (1-2, 6.82 ERA at Durham) maintained his sobriety after concluding the 1994 season in July because of surgery. He returned the following spring and wound up pitching for the Braves' replacement team. When all the players were released or reassigned one day before the games were scheduled to begin, Giard decided to retire prior to having a change of heart and asking to return. Atlanta eventually welcomed him back, but assigned him to Eugene, where he was 3-0 with a 2.38 ERA in 25 games.

Tyler Houston (.244 with four homers and 33 RBIs at Richmond) remained on Atlanta's 40-man roster over the winter and wound up back with the R-Braves for the 1995 season. Serving primarily as a first baseman, his bat continued to show marginal progress, producing at a .255 clip with 12 roundtrippers.

Danny Magee (.272 with 34 RBIs at Macon) showed more signs that he could be Atlanta's next permanent shortstop by hitting .256 and displaying outstanding defensive skills at Durham. An injured arm caused him to miss the last month of the season.

Failing to follow up on his tremendous 1994 season was pitcher Brad Woodall (15-6 with a 2.42 ERA at Richmond). The lefty made the Atlanta roster out of spring training before being returned to Richmond once rosters were trimmed to 25 players in mid-May. His lack of activity in the majors and a lingering foot injury led to a 4-4 record and a 5.10 ERA in 13 games.

The story is equally diverse regarding the players whose names appeared most often in this book.

Mike Birkbeck (13-6 with a 2.73 ERA at Richmond) returned to familiar grounds, only this time it was back in the International League with a former employer, the New York Mets. Starting the year at Norfolk, Birkbeck displayed his consistent form, posting a 5-3 record and a 2.36 ERA before living up to his word and returning to the major leagues. For four starts in late May and early June, the right-hander was the best pitcher the Mets had to offer, his earned run average a paltry 1.63, even though his record stood at 0-1.

As the case had been for several years, Birkbeck was little more than an insurance policy, a stand-in until the Mets deemed their prospects ready. New York went with a youth movement in early June, and sold Birkbeck's contract to Yokohama in Japan. True to form, he missed nary a beat upon crossing the Pacific Ocean, winning his first two decisions with the BayStars.

Prior to his departure for the Far East, in what proved to his final start in the United States, the right-hander scored a run for the first time as a major-leaguer. Realizing the significance of the event, Birkbeck thought a memento would be appropriate and asked umpire Mike Winters, "Can I have the plate?"

In August of 1994, Tim Gillis (.241 with nine homers and 48 RBIs at Greenville) was not unlike his fellow minor-leaguers in that he seemed more a fan than a professional player when asked about the strike. "I miss seeing the highlights every night on *SportsCenter*," said the third baseman. Seven months later, Gillis was thrown in the middle of the situation. Told his lone hope of reaching the majors would come as a member of the replacement team, Gillis suited up and reached Atlanta-Fulton County Stadium for two exhibition games as the squad's best hitter. Released from his contract when the clock struck midnight, Gillis refused an assignment to Greenville as well as a possible opportunity to coach in the farm system. He decided instead to put his business administration degree in computer science to work.

"I want to start a family, and I don't want to be trekking around the minor leagues as a coach with a kid and my wife," Gillis said. "At this point in my life, I'm ready to see what else I have to offer."

John Knott (.287 with 17 homers and 74 RBIs at Macon) got his wish to play winter ball by suiting up for Waverly in the Australian League. After playing for Atlanta's replacement team during spring training, the third baseman also received his long-awaited promotion to Durham, only a year late. Even so, he still proved deserving of a job at the higher level, hitting .267 with 11 home runs.

Mike Mordecai (.280 with 14 home runs and 57 RBIs at Richmond), earned a spot on Atlanta's 40-man roster in November and a job on the 25-man roster in April. His playing time minimal as a rookie reserve, the utility man proved his worth every time he was given a chance. His greatest thrill came in the first round of the National League playoffs, when he drove in the go-ahead run to give Atlanta the victory over Colorado.

"This is what I've been working toward, the realization of a dream," said Mordecai, who hit .280 during the 1995 regular season. "I'm with the Atlanta Braves, playing for the best team in baseball. If I can do that, I can play for any team the majors has to offer."

Matt Murray (9-11 with a 4.34 ERA at Durham and Greenville) felt nearly as exuberant, for 1995 was a year he would never forget. He and his fiancée, Nikki, were wed on February 4, and the right-hander wasted little time rewarding his bride for talking him into continuing his baseball career. Assigned to Greenville after no team picked him up when Atlanta removed the right-hander from the 40-man roster, Murray went 4-0 in five starts with the G-Braves prior to receiving a promotion to Richmond, where he went 10-3 with a 2.78 ERA. He spent two weeks in Atlanta, going 0-2, before being traded to Boston at the end of August.

"I have a lot of mixed feelings," Murray said after learning of the trade. "I always wanted to pitch for Atlanta and I finally did. I guess if I had to be traded, Boston would be the best place to go. Still, it's hard to explain the mixed feelings."

Conversely, the 1995 season began as a nightmare for Carey Paige (10-8 with a 3.40 ERA at Macon and Durham). While wading in the Atlantic Ocean during spring training, the pitcher was hit by a body surfer and suffered sprained ligaments in his knee. He missed more than a month before reporting to Durham in mid-May. After a 5-3 start with the Class A club, Paige was promoted to Greenville and went 1-4 in seven Double-A starts.

"I struggled at Durham before I started throwing strikes and quit worrying about everything else," said Paige, who was acquired by Toronto in the Rule 5 draft after the 1995 season. "It's all about confidence, this whole game. Now I know I can pitch and I know I can get batters out. It's just a matter of doing it every time out."

Terrell Wade (11-5 with a 3.60 ERA between Greenville and Richmond) had a dismal start to the 1995 season before garnering International League player-of-the-week honors with a pair of victories in early June. Still blessed with as much raw talent as anyone in the minors, Wade rebounded to go 10-9 with a 4.56 ERA and received a September promotion to Atlanta.

"I just got to keep doing what I'm doing and I'll be fine," Wade said. "It seems like some people keep waiting for me to slip up. But I feel good about the way I'm going. I feel like I'm right on track to where I want to be."

As disappointing as Wade's start to 1995 was, it paled in comparison to that of Tom Waldrop (.215 with 12 homers and 54 RBIs at Durham). Placed on the disabled list with an injured arm at the end of spring training, the outfielder was sent to Macon, his residence for most of 1993. Upon his return to the active roster in mid-May, Waldrop remained with the South Atlantic League club, but moved little from his position on the bench. By the end of the season, he had been to the plate a mere 194 times, hitting .237 with three home runs and 24 RBIs.

While he survived the off-season cuts made by the Braves, Waldrop had no trouble reading the writing on the wall. Midway through the 1995 slate, the diamond game had become nothing more than something to occupy his time and produce a paycheck until the fall. That's when Waldrop returned to school to finish the two classes he needed for his physical therapy degree. Also in the plans was to marry his girlfriend, Natalie, in November, and begin life without baseball.

"I'm ready to leave it behind," Waldrop said. "Natalie is the reason why I played this year. She told me over the winter that she didn't want me one day to wonder what would've happened if I hadn't given it every opportunity to work out. It's obvious now, and that's fine.

"Some people, some of my teammates, ask me why don't I try to hook on with some other team. It'd be the same way. They would have their pets, the guys who can't necessarily play but the team and a scouting director have their reputation riding on the line. I'm not going to go through that again. I don't want to be like a lot of guys in Triple-A. They're thirty-two years old and still getting jerked around, hoping against hope to get to the majors. I'm twenty-five now, and I did well, better than they ever thought I would when I had a chance to play. I'm pleased with what I did; I just wish I'd been given a chance to do more."

Waldrop took a final drink of his iced tea, glanced around the restaurant on the north side of Macon, then displayed a smile that revealed he understood what took place in major-league organizations and on minor-league fields throughout the country.

"It's funny," Waldrop said. "Your whole life you dream of getting a chance to play professional baseball. Once you get there, you find out this isn't the game you grew up playing in the backyard."

About the Author

Bill Ballew has been covering the progress of the Braves' minor-league players as the Atlanta correspondent for *Baseball America* magazine and other publications since 1991. A frequent guest on radio talk shows throughout the Southeast, the free-lance writer and editor of *Tomahawk*, a monthly publication covering the Atlanta Braves, has had more than 1,000 articles published in more than 30 national and regional magazines since 1988. He received his introduction to the life of minor-league baseball by serving as assistant general manager of the Class A Greenwood Pirates in 1983, his first job after graduating from the University of Georgia's Henry Grady School of Journalism.

Ballew, 34, and his wife, Hope, have a 1-year-old son, Brad. They recently relocated to Asheville, North Carolina, after living eight years in Marietta, Georgia.